Basic Skills

Basic Skills

A Plan for Your Child, A Program for All Children

by

Herbert Kohl

LITTLE, BROWN AND COMPANY   BOSTON · TORONTO

FIRST EDITION

LIBRARY OF CONGRESS CATALOGING IN PUBLICATION DATA

Kohl, Herbert R.
    Basic skills.

    Bibliography: p. 236
    1. Basic education—United States. I. Title.
    LC1035.6.K63   370'.973   81-20869
    ISBN 0-316-50136-0   AACR2

The author is grateful to the following publishers for permission to quote material noted below:

The Transformation of the Schools by Lawrence A. Cremin, Albert A. Knopf, Inc. 1961. Reprinted by permission.

Reprinted by special permission of *Learning*, The Magazine for Creative Teaching, March 1977. © 1977 by Pitman Learning, Inc., 530 University Ave., Palo Alto, CA 94301, for excerpts from "Being Ripped Off? Call A Kid," by Karen Branan and Joe Nathan.

Words as Definitions of Experience by Arnold Wesker, Writers and Readers Cooperative, 1976. Reprinted by permission.

"Bookburning Ceremony by Church School," © 1981 Associated Press. Reprinted by permission.

Report of progress conducted at Norris School, in *Adult Education*, 1938, University of Kentucky, College of Education, Center for Professional Development.

MV

Designed by Janis Capone

*Published simultaneously in Canada
by Little, Brown & Company (Canada) Limited*

PRINTED IN THE UNITED STATES OF AMERICA

For Lou Laub,
whose life has embodied
the principles of democracy

Contents

———

However reluctant one may be to acknowledge the fact, it is none the less certain that the task of trying to educate everybody, which our public schools are engaged in, has proved to be far more difficult than the originators of the idea of such a possibility thought it would be when they set out upon the undertaking.

This is a mild way of stating a most important truth.

Moreover, this truth is steadily forcing its way into general recognition among all classes and conditions of modern society.

All people who are interested in educational affairs are thinking about the situation, and are talking about it constantly, both in private and in public.

Every educational meeting, from a local Teachers' Institute to the annual gathering of the National Educational Association, now makes this condition of affairs the chief subject of its attention, its addresses and discussions.

These facts all prove that the issue of attempting to universalize education is just now one of most intense interest and importance. It follows that, since the whole subject is yet in an unsettled, not to say fermenting, condition, it is open and ready for the most careful study and consideration.

It is because all these things are so that I have written this book, which I hope may help at least a little toward the successful solution of the most momentous problem of the age.

William Hawley Smith,
All of the Children of All of the People, 1912

·INTRODUCTION·

Public Education
and Public Schools

THERE ARE TIMES when I wonder whether my wife and I will finally break down and pull our children out of public school. Many people we know have and I can't think of anyone who hasn't seriously thought about it. It is painful to see one's children wounded or dulled by schooling. Yet there is something about the idea of public education that compels many of us to keep our children in the public schools and work to change them. This same sentiment causes people who decide to put their children in private schools or to educate them at home to feel sad, guilty, and angry, at teachers and administrators who seem powerless to create effective and interesting schools.

Just recently I had a conversation with several parents who were agonizing over whether to pull their children out of our local public school. One of them said quite sadly that she was losing her faith in public education. I pressed and asked what she meant by "faith" in public education. Her response was that faith in public education meant the same thing to her that it meant to her parents and grandparents, that the public schools existed to provide opportunity for all children and that they were part of the dream that America was a land of opportunity for everybody. Loss of faith meant that maybe all children couldn't be educated or that we don't have teachers adequate for the task of educating all the children of all the people. She said the problems of public education seemed overwhelming and she didn't want to see her own children hurt by bad schools. What made her sad and guilty was giving up her grandparents' dreams of equality and opportunity through public education. At the core of her sadness and guilt, and that of many other people, is the acknowledgment

3

that withdrawing one's children from public school represents a loss of faith in democracy, a decision to let parents fend for their own children.

Many of us learned to look at public education as a vehicle for social mobility and economic opportunity. We believed public education was created to provide all the children of all the people with the basic skills necessary for nurturance and participation within a growing democracy. Withdrawal and disillusion, even gritting one's teeth, hanging in, and working to change schools, are acknowledgments that the public schools are not teaching these basic skills.

Over the past five years I've been talking with people about what basic skills they feel should be taught in school and about whether they feel that public schools provided these skills in the past. I've encountered more confusion than clarity, and considerable anger very close to the surface. Some people believe the basics consist of the mechanical aspects of reading, writing, and arithmetic. Others emphasize understanding and creativity. People talked about schools providing students with the skills to deal with "the real world," or about schools providing skills and experiences that lead to personal enrichment. They also talked about schools as models of decent communities. *Basic* meant to people what was basic in their dreams for their own children. One thing that almost everyone expressed was a desire that the public schools return to their former excellence, that we find a way to go back to the basics.

I pushed people on their ideas about this Golden Age of Education, and people acknowledged that if it existed, they hadn't been part of it. Was there ever a time when public schools achieved the goal of providing basic skills to all children? What are those skills? How can they be achieved and how have we gone wrong? These are the questions that have led me to write this book.

I believe in public education but do not believe that the public schools are providing an adequate basic education for our children. It is important to emphasize this distinction between public education and the current state of the public schools, between what could be and what is. We can make a decent system of public education and help our children learn to take control of their lives rather than be managed, controlled, bossed, and bewildered. This book presents a concrete program for the revitalization of public education. It is based on the idea that the fundamental goals of public education should be to develop informed, thoughtful, and sensitive citizens who are able to fulfill their personal needs at the same time that they contribute to making the whole society harmonious and compassionate. We need this wholeness now more than at any time I can remember. It is common to hear people talking about the United States suffering from "too much democracy," "an excess of freedom," and "unbridled liberty." It is time to take a serious look at ourselves and see how much democracy we really have and how far we have to go to achieve the dreams expressed by the Declaration of Independence, which dared to call life, liberty, and the pursuit of happiness rights and not privileges.

The focus of this book is on public education and the struggle to create decent schools for all of our children. I hope it will move people to stay engaged in that effort and to develop concrete programs for action in their own communities. The first section of the book deals with our current problems. What is wrong with the schools and why are we all so frustrated? The schools are being criticized from many different perspectives. Is there a common core of sense in the criticisms leveled by conservative members of the Council on Basic Education, progressives who consider themselves members of the alternative school movement, and just plain frustrated parents? What is the connection between basic skills and life in a democracy, and how are we failing to make it? Why is it that all of the innovations and experiments of the last twenty years have led to frustration, and why is it that the science of education seems to be such a mockery of the natural and physical sciences?

The next section will pursue the cry of "back to the basics" through the history of public education in the United States and try to answer the question raised by Moms Mabley, the comedian: "The good old days, I was there, where was they?" This chapter is the product of a two-year historical search during which I've discovered and rediscovered wonderful American educators such as Elizabeth Peabody, Francis Parker, and Calvin Stowe; have reread such classics as *Uncle Tom's Cabin* and *Little Men* from a new perspective; seen education for the first time woven into the fabric of our history and life. In order to condense over 200 years of history into a single chapter, I decided to use fiction and tell the story of a family of teachers who settled in eastern Ohio just after the Revolutionary War.

The third section is on the relationship between mechanical skills and the content of what is learned. It is an attempt to look at the different ways the three Rs are taught and to formulate some general principles dealing with the goals, content, context, and use of school learning.

The fourth section contains an explicit redefinition of basic skills along with descriptions of how they might be taught. The list has been built from a consideration of good educational practice in the past and the legitimate concerns of parents who see their children in the last part of the twentieth century facing problems that are unique to our stage of technological and social development.

Finally, the book will conclude with practical suggestions about how we can begin to develop a basic-skills program in the public schools in our communities and how we can at the same time create new public centers of learning that can enrich and empower all the children of all the people.

When I began this book over three years ago I was depressed, and tired of fighting to improve public education while witnessing my own children becoming bored and restless. My adventure into our educational past has been revitalizing. For over 200 years many people have cared about children and cared about democracy. The struggle to improve public education is itself a reaffirmation of democratic principles and something we can share with our children. Why not dare to build wonderful places of learning, to imagine and then try to achieve the excellence we have mistakenly placed in the past? The good old days may be ahead of us — there's no harm trying. It's in that spirit that I've articulated a program, one subject to modification and the test of practice, but also one definite enough to provide a starting place for taking up again the task of building an excellent system of public education.

PART ONE

What's Wrong?

THE MOST COMMON COMPLAINTS about our public schools are that students are graduating unable to read, write, or calculate with any proficiency; that respect has disappeared and consequently there are more discipline problems than ever before; that standards are lower than they've ever been; and finally that students don't even care about not having the skills and values that are part of our American heritage.

This analysis of the current state of public education leads many people to the conclusion that schools must return to the basics and occupy themselves with drilling skills, commanding respect, instilling discipline, instituting and enforcing high standards, and strengthening character. Without doing these things, it is argued, the public schools will continue to contribute to the weakening of the moral fiber and strength of our nation. What are needed are harsh solutions to problems conceived in terms of control and obedience. Dress codes, math drills, phonics, corporal punishment shade into each other as inseparable parts of a fantasy solution to genuine problems faced by public education. Yet there is no established connection between learning to read and phonics drill or between the elimination of discipline problems and the use of corporal punishment. Nor is there any substantial evidence that proportionately more students are having discipline problems or failing to learn to read in 1981 than in 1901, 1911, 1921, 1931, or 1971, for that matter.

When it comes to analyzing and solving the problems of public education, I sense a desperate flailing around, an anger and despair that, though justified, is unfocused. There is truth in most people's intuitions about the failure of public education. Too many students are graduating illiterate; there

11

is not enough respect or discipline in the lives of many young people, and there is inadequate appreciation of our national heritage and dreams. Yet we have to be careful not to embrace solutions that intensify these problems. It is important that we take a closer look at current practice in the schools and let our analysis of what is wrong be informed by what is actually happening behind the doors and chain link fences that set schools off from the communities they serve. More important, we must measure our criticisms of the public schools against the purpose of public education, which is to provide the skills and techniques necessary for full participation in a democracy to all the children of all the people in our society.

The dream of free high-quality education is rooted in several fundamental ideas held by the founders of our nation: the ideas that citizenship can be taught, that opportunity must be provided to children of all people if equality and freedom are to be maintained, and that the survival of democracy is dependent upon intelligent, well-educated, and clear-thinking citizens. In our analysis of the current situation, we have to examine whether this fundamental justification for public education is undermined, and whether the lack of democratic practice in the schools may not itself be a significant cause of the problems of public education.

Testing

A good place to begin an analysis of current practice is with the phenomenon of testing. It may be only a slight exaggeration to claim that testing has replaced teaching in most public schools. My own children's school week is framed by pretests, drills, tests, and retests. They know that the best way to read a textbook is to look at the questions at the end of the chapter and then skim the text for the answers. I believe that my daughter Erica, who gets excellent marks, has never read a chapter of any of her school textbooks all the way through, and she's now in the eighth grade.

My children do get occasional relief from testing since some of their teachers have been hired to teach in more open styles, but even they have to prepare their students for mandated state tests and for other classrooms where teachers proudly and openly state they teach to the test.

Teaching to the test is a curious phenomenon. Instead of deciding what skills students ought to learn, helping students learn them, and then using some sensible method of assessment to discover whether students have mastered the skills, teachers are encouraged to reverse the process. First one looks at a commercially available test. Then one distills the skills needed not to master reading, say, or math, but to do well on the test. Finally, the test skills are taught. It is as if the teaching of music were reduced to being able to memorize the notes of a song, or the teaching of driving were limited to practicing the answers on the written driver's license exam. The ability to play music or to drive a car might include those particular skills but is far from equivalent to them. In the same way, the ability to read or write or calculate might imply the ability to do reasonably well on standardized tests. However, neither reading, writing, nor arithmetic develop simply through being taught to take tests. We must be careful to avoid mistaking preparation for a test of a skill with the acquisition of that skill. Too many discussions of basic skills make this fundamental confusion because people are test obsessed rather than concerned with the nature and quality of what is taught.

Test obsession may even cause educational problems. Recently many schools have faced what could be called the crisis of comprehension or, in simple terms, the phenomenon of students with phonic and grammar skills still being unable to understand what they read. These students are competent at test taking and filling in workbooks and ditto masters. However they have little or no experience reading or thinking, and talking about what they read. They know the details but can't see or understand the whole. They are taught to be so concerned with grades that they have no time or ease of mind to think about meaning, and reread things if necessary.

Teaching to the test instead of teaching children is a defensive strategy for teachers, especially in situations where students are bored or where the evaluation of teachers is based on students' test scores. If you can arrange for enough students to be test-wise so that your class looks good on paper, you can feel secure that you'll get a positive evaluation. Moreover, many bored children (mine included) can be controlled by the threat of bad grades and can be kept busy memorizing and copying so they will do reasonably well on tests. My children don't worry much about what they're learning. What is important is how they are doing. Content has been sacrificed for control too often in their school experience.

Some children cannot be controlled by tests and fail or even refuse to participate in the process. The tests provide another protection for teachers in these cases. Failure on tests is often confused with lack of intelligence, and blame for failure is shifted from poor teaching methods and impoverished content to students or their parents. This shift is especially common in schools that serve children of the poor where massive failure on standardized tests is often taken as proof of parental neglect or the inferior intelligence of a whole community.

The confusion of intelligence, achievement, culture, and educability dates back to the first intelligence tests. These tests were designed to sort people out according to their innate intelligence, and were based upon beliefs that some groups of people are more intelligent than other groups. The notion of standardized tests arose in the distinctly undemocratic climate of the growth of the British Empire under Queen Victoria.

The idea of developing a test for intelligence originated

with Sir Francis Galton, who, in his book *Hereditary Genius*, published in 1869, hypothesized that people differ from each other in general ability by measurable amounts and constructed an imaginary scale for the distribution of intelligence using a normal curve.* This *assumption* of a normal distribution of intelligence and ability underlies most test construction. Tests are made to produce normally distributed scores.

It may seem trivial to dwell on this last fact, but it is easy to lose sight of the fact that people, individuals, with their own biases and cultural baggage, *construct* tests. Behind claims for the objectivity of tests are assumptions such as the one about the normal distribution of intelligence. One could just as well assume intelligence is distributed bimodally

or skewed toward one pole or another. For example, if you believe that a small number of people are born with brains that don't function effectively, and a smaller number with some form of genius, but that most people are born with the capacity to be quite intelligent, the intelligence curve would look something like this:

Deficient   Normal   Quite Intelligent   Genius

Of course, this curve isn't as aesthetically pleasing or balanced as a normal curve but it might be more accurate. One could certainly build tests assuming this skewed distribution of intelligence.

* A normal curve is shaped like a bell. Because of its shape it is also called a bell curve. A normal distribution represented by such a curve clusters most scores about the middle [(2) normal] range, and falls off uniformly toward the left [(1) inferior] and right [(3) superior] sides, with 50 percent of people falling in the middle and 25 percent on each side.

The assumption of the normal distribution implies that some people have superior intelligence, that most people are average, and that some are inferior. The use of the words "superior" and "inferior" occur throughout the early literature on testing and give rise to the suspicion that the development of tests may have some social and political dimensions.

In considering the role standardized testing plays in current disputes over basic skills and the effectiveness of public education, there are several things that must be kept in mind. First, the tests are constructed to create a hierarchy of success and failure rather than to determine the competency of individuals. Test items are designed by educational psychologists and then tested out on a small sample of students. If questions are easily answered by all the students, more difficult ones are added to the next version of the test. If the questions are all too hard, easy questions are added. Through trial and error a test is built so that the results will conform to a normal curve of achievement. This implies that some students must be expected to fail; that a certain amount of failure is normal. In fact, half the students should fall below the norm if the class were to fit the model of a normal distribution of achievement. Remember the normal curve divides a group in half and falls off at the ends:

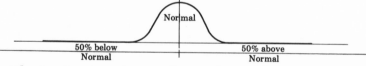

The implication of normed tests then is that one should be content with a group average on or above the norm. For many teachers this is equivalent to the belief that many students will naturally be below the norm. Failure is no big thing except in the lives of individuals. The tests, instead of raising standards, often have the practical effect of giving teachers justification for the failure of many of their students and excuses for not working harder to help students who aren't learning.

Add to the acceptance of failure as a way of life (a distinctly undemocratic notion that in many ways is equivalent to the idea that the poor will always be with us) the cultural linguistic bias of the test makers and the confusion of achievement with intelligence, and what results is a school situation in which some failure is considered inevitable. When students fail it is their problem. For some reason or another it is their nature to be below the norm. It is easy to forget, in a test-dominated, norm-ridden situation, that the mission of the public schools is to teach and not to sort out students. Failure cannot be taken for granted in a democracy.*

Teachers Don't Teach Anymore

A great deal of parental anger directed at public schools is a consequence of teachers' and administrators' resignation to the failure of many students. One constantly hears complaints about teachers who won't teach and statements about how teachers in the past made sure their students learned. There is truth in those assertions. The current test obsession institutionalizes failure and makes it possible for teachers to minimize the demands they make upon themselves and their students. What I see happening in public schools is the acceptance of what could be called the testing mentality. Learning programs are nothing more than testing programs. If the average performance of a class is on or above the constructed norm, the teacher is covered and the students below the norm are educationally handicapped, culturally deprived, or, in less polite terms, dumb. As one teacher told me, "There's nothing you can do about the dummies except put them in a special class. They're not my problem."

"They're not my problem." That statement itself is a concise expression of the problem. In a system dominated by so-called objective tests, scientifically developed skills pro-

* See Appendix for a more detailed discussion of the nature and history of testing.

grams, and text- and workbooks that are designed like tests, who is responsible for the children who have not learned? And who is responsible for making learning interesting and challenging for students who, though they do well on tests, are bored and resentful? As one parent said to me, "Where are the teachers these days?"

I've pressed people on what they believe teachers used to do and what isn't being done now. The most common answers were that teachers used to take time to explain things, that they didn't give up so easily on students who had learning problems, and that they spent time trying to help you develop what you were interested in. Supposedly, they also knew how to handle discipline problems and maintain respect. Underlying all the answers was a belief that teachers used to care about children and believe in their potential, and that somehow the public schools now didn't have any faith in the students. There was a strong feeling that students were being blamed for the schools' failure and that it just wasn't fair to blame the victims of poor teaching for their boredom or failure.

Testing is just one facet of the more general aspect of current public education that could be called the victimization of the client. Parents send their children to public schools to learn, and then if the children fail or become bored, the children and families are blamed. The recurrent questions that people raised to me were, "What is the responsibility of the schools? What can we expect them to do for our children? Why do they blame us for their failures?"

Consider, for example, a twelve-year-old who has not learned how to read. There are a number of ways to approach him. One way is to assume that since reading is basic in our society it's important to find a way to enable that person to read. The educational task would be the same as helping a nonliterate fifty-year-old learn to read. It's as simple as that: X can't read, we have to figure out, with the help of X, how to help him get power over the written word. No question of retardation, disturbance, or failure enters. It's a simple matter of fitting learning and teaching together. After all, many societies have developed successful adult literacy programs, and throughout our history we have also developed many programs that taught immigrants and other nonliterate adults to read and write. The assumption of all these programs was that the students could learn and that it was possible to be intelligent and not have learned how to read.

There is another way to approach the same twelve-year-old, which could be called *blaming the student for the failure of the school.* This hypothetical young man is in the sixth grade, a seven-year veteran of the school. For six of those seven years he has been placed in the same reading program and failed. He even got left behind once to repeat lessons he already failed with a teacher who was unable to assist him. By the end of seven years he is indifferent to worksheets, has no motivation to do well on tests. Yet if you ask, he will say that reading is important, and might even apologize for being a failure. The student is turned from a person who has not learned to read into an educational problem. Because the system is rigid and hierarchical, creativity in teaching has been replaced by ingenuity in categorization. The system doesn't have to change; the child is deficient. That's what makes parents angry and often leads to them pulling their children out of public schools. There is a lot of feeling that teachers are blaming students for failure that should be blamed on the school.

Blaming the Students

Here are some common professional explanations of student failure:

· These children can't learn because of their background.
· These children can't learn because of their poverty and cultural deprivation.
· This child can't read because he's dyslexic.

- This child can't read because she's hyperactive and has minimum brain dysfunction.

In these cases an educational problem is shifted to some other structure: the structure of the community, the culture, or the brain of the child. Educational problems are translated into noneducational terms, tests are used to validate the diagnoses, and solutions are looked for in modifying those external structures. A closer look at these statements reveals how they are simply attempts to avoid the democratic responsibility for teaching the widest number of children possible by playing at pseudosociology and pseudoscience.

These children can't learn because of their background. There is no clear connection between learning and background. This becomes clear when you quantify the general claim and get specific claims like:

These children can't learn to add because of their background
OR
These children can't learn to read simple words because of their background.

People from every conceivable background learn to add and read, despite poverty, language differences, cultural and psychological differences. That has been part of the power of public education in our past. The learning problems are more likely caused by the ways school life relates to the child's culture, which is a complex matter that differs from culture to culture.

A version of the background argument is:

These children can't learn because of their poverty and cultural deprivation. Many people have been proud of their ability to read despite being poor. Many people have not learned to read because teachers, believing this myth, have given up on teaching the children of the poor. This is not to minimize the cruel and devastating effects of poverty but simply to point out that one can be poor, demoralized, and oppressed, and still learn to read, especially if reading is felt to have some liberating power.

In addition, it is necessary not to confuse poverty with cultural deprivation. To be culturally deprived is, perhaps, to have your own culture stolen from you or to be isolated from all contact with people of your own group, or to live in a world where cultural forms change faster than they can be assimilated. There are people who are poor and yet culturally rich, and others who are rich and confused about the culture they belong to.

> *This child can't read because he's dyslexic*
> *AND*
> *This child can't learn because she's hyperactive and has*
> *minimal brain dysfunction.*

Consider the following equivalencies to understand these two tautologies:

1. *Dyslexic* means can't read.
2. *Hyperactive* means moves around, which implies not sitting down and learning when told, which leads the professional to infer minimal brain damage, which is called hyperactivity.

These cruel tautologies have caused many children unreasonable pain. They rest on the assumption that any learning problem is the child's fault (perhaps an echo of the sentiment that the poor desire to be poor, because they haven't worked hard enough). Resistance to school authority or confusion over what is being taught can lead to a child's being categorized as educationally handicapped or as having a learning disability. Thousands of perfectly normal children are treated in this way as if they have some kind of intellectual cancer and need special treatment. In fact, drugs, as unproven in their effectiveness as laetrile, are being forced on children in unprecedented numbers. In some school districts as many as 25 percent of the students are forced to take Ritalin as a condition of attendance at public school. The effect of Ritalin on learning and behavior is not known, though in many cases it induces passivity and lassitude in formerly alert and active youngsters.[1]

The control of behavior is accepted as a substitute for creative teaching. Test results are used to substantiate the stigmatization of some students, and the need to drill students in so-called basic skills is used to mask the more desperate attempt to control students' behavior. Given the common confusion of intelligence and achievement, teachers have usually given up on the students they consign to special education. Many of those students have also given up on themselves academically (it's easy to believe you are sick if you're treated as if you have a disease). These same students, however, strike back in other ways. It's hard to love an institution that punishes you. Humiliation leads to anger and retaliation. Students who are humiliated in the classroom, who are made to look "dumb" by the tests, and are put in "dummy" classes, should not be expected to be loyal, faithful, and respectful. Discipline problems are usually created within the school rather than brought to the school from home or the streets.

Violence

Fear of violence in the public schools is another reason people withdraw their children from public school. Too many schools have become fields of battle between students and teachers. This is a consequence of a system with built-in failure, staffed by demoralized, frustrated people. Even caring teachers express anger and depression over demands made by constant testing, paperwork, and bureaucratic regulation. Often this anger is taken out on the student, which in turn leads to student anger and, at times, violence. It's a vicious cycle. The teacher and student are both trapped in a system that is not working for either of them, and yet they have no power to change the whole.

Violence in schools is a direct consequence of the distinctly unloving and undemocratic way young people are treated. When students are channeled into special classes, given drugs, labeled hyperactive, handicapped, or dyslexic, we have in essence abandoned them and created in the school a substantial underclass that has to hate the institution.

I remember a story the student-body president of a high school I ran in Berkeley told me of her life in the educational underworld. Christine was tall, even in the first grade, and had a wry sense of humor and a stubborn streak. When she was in the fourth grade, someone stole a five-dollar bill from a student in her class. The teacher insisted on searching everyone's desk and purse. Christine refused to let her purse be searched and told the teacher that the only condition under which the purse could be searched was if Christine could search the teacher's purse. Then if a five-dollar bill were found in either purse they'd know who was the thief. Christine's purse was empty and she knew that most likely the teacher's purse contained a five-dollar bill. The teacher exploded, Christine resisted, and before she knew it she was in the psychologist's office, and in a week was transferred to a class for hyperactive, educationally handicapped students. She said she didn't mind the class for a while — it was a good place to read, and she loved to read romantic novels. For three years she put up with being handicapped. Then one day when she was in the seventh grade she got fed up with being talked to as if she were sick or retarded, tired of, as she put it, being given juice and graham crackers every morning at ten as if she were in kindergarten or in a hospital. She grabbed the pitcher from her teacher, bounced it off his head, and walked out of school. She didn't return until four years later when her brother urged her to enroll at our high school.

Christine's story is not atypical. Between 10 and 40 percent of the students at just about any public school are labeled as handicapped, treated as if they're ill, instead of being taught well, and are being pushed into violent thoughts, if not actions. The schools create the situation of violence that then causes people to lose faith in them.

The School as Adversary

The whole business of educational handicapping is counter to the democratic traditions that led to public education in the first place. The goal of school should be to seek ways to teach skills to the largest number of students. Instead we find ourselves with institutions run largely on prison or mental-hospital models. Students must attend school and must do as they are told once they are inside the door. They are sure to be punished if they raise questions, try to make decisions, or suggest different ways of going about learning. There is an adversary relationship between the people who work for the institution and the people served by the institution.

This adversary relationship extends beyond students to parents and other members of the community and accounts for much of the bitterness directed at the public schools. Teachers, administrators, and other educational experts claim professional knowledge, professional prerogatives, and professional salaries. No matter what you know, you have to be a credentialed teacher to teach in the schools, a credentialed administrator to be a principal, a credentialed psychologist to make statements about children's minds, a Ph.D. in educational psychology to do valid research in education. Yet despite all these credentials and the apparatus surrounding qualification and certification, people outside do not see a smoothly running, effective institution serving the needs of children. Instead, what most of us perceive is an inverse relationship between claims of professionalism and student performance. The more credentials, the less learning. That's the way it feels to most people. The number of students defined as handicapped grows, boredom pervades the schools, and in that demoralized context professional attitudes look like ways of avoiding responsibility for teaching the basic skills that will help young people become effective adults and decent citizens.

Concerns over the acquisition of these basic skills is at the center of the current hostility toward public schools. People feel that they pay for the schools and that the schools should have the responsibility to teach the children. It is not the children's or their parents' responsibility to know how to teach. People have told me over and over again, "Why should we pay them if they can't teach?" That statement is at the core of the movements for alternative schools, fundamentalist schools, and every other variety of private education. Testing, categorizing, grading, sorting, all represent a professional abandonment of faith in people's ability to learn. They imply an abandonment of the notion that schools exist for the children, and that public education can provide skills that will give every child the opportunity to achieve a full and nurturing adult life. What is wrong with the schools can be summarized quite simply: They appear to be against, not for, our children, and therefore we must ask if we need them.

·PART TWO·

Back to Basics

FREE PUBLIC EDUCATION that will provide opportunity for all children in our country is part of the American dream. My grandparents came to this country not so much because of what it could offer them as for what it could offer their children. To this day my father tries to repay his college and other schools he attended for the free education they provided him. He swears by what used to be, and yet admits at times that all the schools of his day weren't that good and that there were schools he attended that were no different from the public schools now. However, he and many, many people believe in the good old days of public education when all students learned the skills they needed for adult life.

People want to believe in the good old days. It is an assertion of the belief that there was a time when all the institutions of American democracy functioned smoothly and that current problems are just temporary aberrations. Regarding the schools, it is a reassertion of the idea that every child should have the opportunity to be successful in life. When we cease to believe in democracy, we lose faith in ourselves as a nation. Our strength is not ultimately the strength of our weapons or propaganda. It will only come from our ability to realize the democratic dreams of the people who struggled in the eighteenth century to make us a nation.

At times of loss of faith — and we are experiencing a loss of faith in institutions like the public schools, which are essential to our ideas of ourselves as a nation — it is comfortable to turn to the past. The cry of "back-to-the-basics" is a plea for a return to democratic ideas, for a return to times of opportunity and optimism. Yet, what happened back there? As Benjamin Rush, one of the signers of the Declaration of Independence and the founder of the first antislavery society in the United States, said in 1787:

> There is nothing more common than to confound the terms of *American Revolution* with those of the late *American War*. The American war is over, but this is far from being the case with the American revolution. On the contrary, nothing but the first act of the great drama is closed.[2]

One central theme of Act Two of the American Revolution was the development of free basic education. We did not begin with any models. Free public education was invented in the United States, and it is worth going back to that post-revolutionary moment when education was considered essential to the development of an American democracy. The basics had to be defined and turned into programs. What was to be basic for education in a democracy? People have never agreed upon an answer and that is a question we have been struggling with for over 200 years. It is worth taking a look at where we have been in order to illuminate where we are and what we need to do in the next twenty-five years to revitalize public education and reaffirm our faith in democracy.

Over the last three years I've been trying to discover when the "back" in the phrase "back to the basics" happened. When was that time when all children were well behaved, learned the basics, and graduated from school successful effective citizens? I never did find such a time but did discover that the struggle to create democratic schools has been a central theme of our national history and that disagreements about what kind of schools we should create predate the Constitution and Declaration of Independence. The adventure into our educational past has been exciting and I find it impossible to condense all that I've learned into one chapter. In order to give a sense of that history, however, I've created a fiction, a story of an American teaching family (there are actually many teaching families) that struggled

to build public education from the beginning of our existence as a nation. All of the facts in the chapter are accurate
and there is a bibliographic essay on my sources in the Bibliography. What I have tried to do in the chapter is capture
the spirit of the struggle to create public education, and
through that, to ensure democracy in our nation. Catherine
Drinker Bowen, in her essay *The Writing of Biography*
(page 8), described the kind of history that I have created
for Turin, Ohio, a fictional town somewhere in Eastern Ohio
near the Pennsylvania border:

> The facts on which my narrative is based are available to
> everyone. I aim not to startle with new material but to per-
> suade with it, and I have chosen the narrative form because
> for me it is the most persuasive . . . I have drawn a portrait
> . . . I studied the available evidence and on the basis of it,
> built pictures which to me are consistent with the evidence.[3]

Education in Turin: A Fictional Narrative

All of the old Pennsylvania people claimed an acquain-
tance with Benjamin Franklin, but Elizabeth believed that
her grandfather, Jonathan Stokes, was the only one whose
stories were convincing enough to make it plausible. Elizabeth was a teacher and loved to hear her grandfather tell
teaching tales.

Jonathan Stokes was born in Philadelphia in 1760. In 1776
at the age of sixteen he joined the Pennsylvania militia on
their mad march to Amboy, New Jersey, to support Washington's effort to hold New York. He was wounded in the
right leg and, as his friends used to joke, limped his way
through the whole Revolutionary War.

Stokes was one of Philadelphia's seasonal soldiers. During
the winters from 1777 to 1783 he apprenticed as a printer.
During the springs and summers he fought with the Pennsylvania militia, which by the end of war was as good a
fighting unit as any in the world.

After the war, Jonathan Stokes worked as a printer in

Philadelphia, trying to scrape enough money together to buy his own press and type and set himself up as a printer. It was during that time, he told anyone who would listen, that he met Franklin. He had been invited by another printer to join the Leather Apron for an evening of discussion at a local tavern.

The Leather Apron was the name adopted by members of the self-education group set up by Benjamin Franklin to distinguish themselves from the Merchants' Every Night, which was composed of older and richer citizens, and the Bachelors, which was a drinking club. Franklin's group, whose formal name was the Junto, consisted of working people — joiners, printers, surveyors, shoemakers — who were serious about science, politics, education, community service, and, in its early years, revolution.

The Junto met once a week in a local tavern. Questions were set for study and research for the next meeting, and then the previous week's questions were discussed, with occasional pauses for toasts and rounds of ale. Jonathan Stokes said that what delighted him most about Franklin's circle was the combination of humor and seriousness. They discussed questions such as "Whence comes the Dew that stands on the outside of a Tankard that has cold Water in it in the Summer Time?" . . . "If a Sovereign Power attempts to deprive a Subject of his Right (or which is the same thing, of what he thinks is his Right) is it justifiable in him to resist if he is able?" . . . "Does it not in a general Way require a great Study and intense Application for a Poor Man to become rich and Powerful, if he would do it, without the Forfeiture of his Honesty?"[4] In the midst of these discussions they joked, drank, and brought up proposals for their mutual assistance and for ways of aiding the Philadelphia community. It was through these discussions that the idea of a public lending library grew, and through their reverence for the printed word that Jonathan learned the importance of building up and sharing a collection of books.

One of Jonathan's prized possessions was a copy of Benjamin Franklin's *Proposals Relating to the Education of Youth in Pennsylvania.* It was hard to get a copy as it was printed in 1749, but Jonathan was able to trade an older printer several evenings' work for a copy. The education of the young was one of Jonathan's obsessions though he had no formal schooling himself. In a way he was relieved he didn't have to attend the schools he observed, as they treated students harshly and didn't encourage the boldness and inventiveness Jonathan believed the new nation needed. He found a footnote in Franklin's book that struck something deep within him and he memorized it. The footnote was a quote from a Mr. Hutcheson, who was a professor in Glasgow during the 1690s:

> The principal end of education is, to form us wise and good creatures, useful to others, and happy ourselves. The whole art of education lies within a narrow compass, and is reducible to a very simple practice; namely, to assist in unfolding those natural and moral powers with which man is endowed, by presenting proper objects and occasions; to watch their growth that they be not diverted from their end, or disturbed in their operation by any foreign violence; and gently to conduct and apply them to all the purposes of private and public life.[5]

There was a lot of movement west in the 1790s. People like Jonathan Stokes felt constrained on the East Coast. There were too many printers in Philadelphia, too little opportunity. Ohio was opening up, growing, might even become a state. The Stokes family moved to eastern Ohio and settled in the small town of Turin (pronounced *Tour in* by the settlers).

The town had been settled by people from Connecticut, though it had Virginians who had fought in Ohio during the war, some French people, remnants of the Indian communities, a small number of free blacks, and a recent influx of Pennsylvania migrants. People kept to their own kind and their own churches. Jonathan, because he was the only printer in town, knew almost everybody. He printed notices, stationery, advertisements, posters. His shop sold books, soap, candles, and was also the town post office. After a while it seemed natural that he be town clerk when, in 1802, Ohio became a state and things began to get a bit more formal. By virtue of being town clerk, another job, that of superintendent of schools, became Jonathan's. There was no school bureaucracy in those days and in many communities no public schools. The town clerk assumed all the responsibilities for administering public services, including the schools.

Stokes spent more and more time on school matters. He set up a small group like Franklin's Junto, only associated with the Society of Freemasons. They worked to develop a school and small lending library in Turin. They encountered many problems, especially with the school. Some church people didn't approve of mixing children together. Others worried about whether the secular teachings of the Freemasons and nondenominational deists would be part of the curriculum. Then there was the problem of what to do with the children of the free slaves, and of the demands of immigrants from western Pennsylvania who wanted their children to be taught in German.

The creation of free public schools for all the children, raised in Turin, as it did throughout the nation, all the complex problems of how a democracy could be forged out of such a mixture of nations, races, and classes.

Jonathan Stokes was surprised and delighted when his granddaughter Elizabeth, who was just sixteen, volunteered to teach at the first public school in Turin. Elizabeth was almost as old as the new century, born in 1812. She was considered a special child. Her grandfather remarked that she must have come into the world reading, and always reminded her that Benjamin Franklin used to comment that he never remembered a time when he couldn't read.

Elizabeth used to spend hours in her grandfather's library, and by the time she was eleven she discussed all the questions brought up at the Masons' meetings with him. She took care of her cousins and younger brothers and sisters and felt that teaching, having fun with children, and exploring the world were some of the things she enjoyed doing most. A footnote from that book by Benjamin Franklin that her grandfather always quoted stuck with her and formed the basis of her teaching when she took charge of the one-room school at Turin in 1828:

> I say that even children are capable of studying nature, for they have eyes and don't want curiosity; they ask questions, and love to be informed; and here we need only awaken and keep up in them the desire of learning and knowing, which is natural to all mankind. Besides this study, if it is to be called a study, instead of being painful and tedious, is pleasant and agreeable . . . it is inconceivable how many things children are capable of, if all the opportunities of instructing them were laid hold of, with which they themselves supply us.[6]

Elizabeth began her work in a small shed behind the print shop/post office. Her one regret was that the four black children in Turin were excluded from the school, but she hoped when she was older that she could do something about that. She was committed to the development of common schools, of free schools for all children. She considered herself liberal and enlightened, and valued having children read and learn to think. Reading was a way to keep up with developments in the larger world, and to develop the spirit of inquiry. For her as for Franklin and other early Americans, an inquiring mind was a powerful tool in a new country where one's opportunities were only limited by one's intelligence and diligence.

As soon as twenty families supported her work, she requested that they build her a schoolhouse. The one-room school was built with donated labor and furniture, and was supported by income from the sale of the land set aside by the federal government in Ohio's statehood charter to support public education. The school was, for many people in the community, a symbol that their dream of a democratic society would be realized, through education, by their children and grandchildren.

The other school in town was more fundamentalist. It grew out of a sectarian, traditionalist church. As John Clayton, the teacher, put it, "The role of education is to instill respect for the Bible, discipline, and the spirit of hard work." John's school started in the home of his brother, a minister, and then moved to the social hall of the newly constructed church. In 1827, when a school tax of one dollar a year on each householder was established, John also asked the parents of the children he served to build a schoolhouse. As was quite common at the time, two one-room schools were built in different parts of the community.

John and Elizabeth had different notions of what common schools should be, and their work reflected those differences, though both were highly respected in the community.

The atmosphere of Elizabeth's school was informal, more like a home than a formal place of learning. She had students who ranged in age from seven to sixteen help each other and take responsibility for keeping the school in good repair. Elizabeth read novels to her students and kept them up on local and national political events. Her family were abolitionists and every year she taught lessons on the evils of slavery. She told her students that she vowed to take in a free black student one day even though state law prohibited mixed schools.

Elizabeth had been teaching for almost ten years when something happened that changed her life. In 1836, Calvin Stowe, then a professor at the Western Literary Institute and College of Professional Teachers in Cincinnati, had been sent to study schools in Europe by the Ohio state legislature. Stowe was born in 1802, the year of Ohio's admission into the Union. As Stowe said in his report to the legislature,

In some of the old communities of central Europe, where it happened to be known that I was born in the same year in which Ohio became a sovereign state, it seemed to be a matter of amusement as well as gratification, that a man who was just as old as the state in which he lived, had come with official authority to inquire respecting the best mode of education for the growing population of his native land; and they remarked that our Governor and Legislators must be very enlightened and highly cultivated men.[7]

The Report on Elementary Public Instruction in Europe was submitted to the Thirty-sixth General Assembly of the State of Ohio, December 19, 1837. Ten thousand copies of the report were printed and distributed to every school district in the state. In the report, Stowe urged the establishment of common schools throughout Ohio and said:

Shall this object (of creating an excellent free system of education), then, so desirable in itself, so entirely practicable, so easily within our reach, fail of accomplishment? For the honor and welfare of our state, for the safety of our whole nation, I trust it will not fail; but that soon we shall witness in this commonwealth the introduction of a system of common school instruction, fully adequate to all the wants of our population.[8]

The Stowe report was received in Turin late in 1837 by Jonathan Stokes, the town clerk and superintendent of schools. He gave it to Elizabeth before reading it himself. She sat down to read it one night and came to the realization, like many teachers in the 1830s and '40s, that what she had been doing intuitively was part of a tradition to democratize societies through the schools that dated back to Europe in the seventeenth century and perhaps even earlier. She also learned from Stowe that a great deal had been written about educational theory and practice that she had no access to. She was determined to learn more about education and improve her practice and decided to spend a summer in Cincinnati at the Western Literary Institute and

College of Professional Teachers where Stowe and his colleagues were offering a summer teachers institute.

Cincinnati changed Elizabeth's life, or at least that's what she always said. At the institute she met Stowe himself and his father-in-law, Lyman Beecher. The whole Beecher family overwhelmed her with their fervor and their eccentricity. In Catherine Beecher, Lyman's oldest child, she met the most remarkable woman she'd ever encountered. They took walks together and Catherine convinced her of the importance of education for women. Elizabeth's first interest in women's issues came through the Beechers, and though later on she felt Catherine put too much emphasis on the domestic role of the woman, she always read Catherine's books and attended her lectures whenever possible.

Henry Ward, one of the sons, impressed her with the eloquence of his language and the vehemence with which he opposed slavery. Harriet, Calvin Stowe's wife, was more reflective, a born writer. Elizabeth remembered years later that it seemed natural to her that Harriet would write a book that would make her world famous and change society at the same time. Her copy of *Uncle Tom's Cabin*, which she sent east and got Harriet to autograph, was one of her most prized possessions. She gave it to her daughter Alice when years later Alice decided to become a teacher, and pointed out her favorite quote from the book, "Your little child is your only true democrat."

It was not only the people that Elizabeth met that had such a profound influence on her. It was the names she heard and the books she discovered. There was Rousseau's *Emile;* there were the works of Pestalozzi, the great Swiss educator, who taught children of the poor; and there were the works of Froebel, the German who created gardens for children, *kindergartens.* She was particularly struck by Froebel's ideas about the importance of play in learning. She had seen children learn through play and experimentation but hadn't articulated the importance of these processes for herself.

When she returned to Turin she transcribed in a flowing and graceful hand a quote from Froebel and hung it up behind her desk. The quote read:

> Play is the first means of development of the human mind, its first effort to make acquaintance with the outward world, to collect original experiences from things and facts, and so exercise the powers of body and mind.[9]

Froebel and Pestalozzi weren't only interesting educationally. Elizabeth sensed in their work the same dream as the one that kept her teaching rather than raising a family of her own. The children could make democracy happen.

Elizabeth returned to Turin in the fall of 1838 with a renewed sense of the importance of her work. She told her students stories about what she had learned, organized a women's group to discuss issues of education pertaining to women, and became an even more ardent abolitionist.

Elizabeth wasn't the only educator in Turin who had encountered new ideas. John Clayton, the teacher at the church school, learned of the American Sunday School Movement and traveled to Philadelphia to meet John P. Crozer and spend time at his Baptist Sunday School. Crozer and other ministers were strong proponents of public support for education. However, they believed that public education should also be Christian education and that the United States should become a Christian democracy based as much upon the Bible as on the Constitution. They suspected deists like Horace Mann, the Stowes, and Beechers who, though professed Christians, didn't believe in received authority and put too much emphasis on thinking things out for themselves.[10]

When John returned to Turin he convinced his congregation that their school should be a Christian public school and they applied for public funds, forcing Elizabeth for the first time to break her uneasy truce with John. The fight over God in the schools was fought in Turin and throughout the country in the 1830s, '40s, and '50s, and resulted in Turin as in most places in an uneasy compromise. John's school received some tuition reimbursement in exchange for conceding to Elizabeth's school the title Turin Common School.

During the late 1840s and the '50s, Elizabeth devoted much of her time to the abolitionist cause, and when the Fugitive Slave Law was passed on 18 September 1850, she offered the basement of her house to the Underground Railroad. By then Elizabeth had ceased teaching and gotten married. It was sad for her to give up the school. She had been teaching since she was sixteen and informally even before that. But as she entered her thirties she realized that new things were stirring within her. Even though it was uncommon for a woman over thirty to marry, she wanted a child of her own, a family, and at that time it was considered inappropriate for married women to teach. A widower, a friend of her brother's, proposed and she accepted. She had to give up her children to have a child. She also wanted to work with adults, to teach people about the impossibility of having slavery within a true democracy. She wanted to develop higher educational opportunities for women, and one time persuaded Catherine Beecher to come to Turin to talk to their woman's group. Her school was taken over by one of her students who had attended a professional teachers college.

The late 1840s and the 1850s were a time of turmoil. The issue of slavery and division of the North and the South were becoming increasingly painful. After the abortive revolutions in Europe in 1848, many European educators and revolutionaries migrated to the United States, and many German-speaking ones settled in Ohio where there already was a substantial German population. These forty-eighters carried many of Froebel's, Pestalozzi's, and Rousseau's ideas to the United States, and may people heard about kindergartens for the first time from them.

In 1851, kindergartens were banned in Prussia as being

revolutionary. Froebel, an old man by this time, was heart-broken but dreamed of developing kindergartens in the United States, a place where the dream of democracy was still alive. Elizabeth remembered hearing Elizabeth Peabody, the sister-in-law of Horace Mann, a Froebelian and leading American educator, lecture on Froebel and was particularly struck by some of Froebel's last words. He said to his companion, the Countess von Bulow, "Now if people will not recognize and support my cause in my native land I will go to America, where a new life is freely unfolding itself and a new education of man will find a footing.[11]

The Civil War was a trauma. In Turin there were many Southern sympathizers, and Elizabeth's educational ideas and her politics were lumped together as subversive. She was a staunch Unionist but saw beyond the issues of North versus South to more fundamental issues of economics. She had befriended one of the forty-eighters and learned of the works of Karl Marx. She strongly disagreed, felt he was too atheistic and violent. Yet there was a truth to his analysis she couldn't deny. Slavery was an economic issue in the South as well as a human one, and perhaps the economic explanation could account for the acceptance of slavery by many otherwise decent people. Marx confused and angered her because he called into question the fundamental importance she placed on education.

Elizabeth's daughter, Alice, a late and only child, was born just before the Civil War. She grew up during the misery of the war, and the confusion and demoralization that followed it. Her mother tried to protect her from many of the horrors, but it was impossible not to experience the physical and psychological scars the war left on its participants. Turin, divided during the war, had a particular need of a healing time and Elizabeth decided to do something. There were so many problems, she decided to focus on those she knew best, those relating to the common schools.

The town experienced an influx of blacks from the South

whose education had to be provided for. There were also new migrations from Pennsylvania, New England, and Europe. By 1868 the potential student population was near 150, too large to be accommodated in a one-room school or the Christian School. If the community was to build a new school, there had to be some way to reconcile all the differences that existed in the community. Elizabeth, with the assistance of the teachers at both schools, convened a series of town forums on education quite unaware of what she was opening up. On the first night parents from the fundamentalist school came in a large group. Some members of the business community attended, as well as several of the farmers from the surrounding area. A handful of parents from Elizabeth's former school also came. Only two black adults came. They were friends of Elizabeth's and came more as a favor to her than out of their own conviction. The racism that was generated by the defeat of the South and the influx of blacks led most blacks in Turin to keep to themselves for safety.

Elizabeth was her usual romantic self. She believed people could solve problems, that one school could be created that would be excellent and satisfy the community. Her black friends and her Marxist friend as well could have told her differently, but she wouldn't have listened anyway.

From the outset the meeting was dominated by representatives of the business community. They expressed concern about building a new school when the community already had two school buildings and some informal arrangements for blacks in community homes. After all, the population could decrease and leave an empty building. There were many arguments against a new building. However, an eloquent plea by both teachers almost convinced the business people that it would be in the children's and town's best interest to build a new school. Only . . . No one wanted to say the *only*, but at last, in a hesitant way, one of the farmers suggested that it would be possible to save money and solve a problem by giving one of the old schools to the local blacks. With the exception of Elizabeth and her friends, everyone was relieved. The town could have a school, blacks would have a school. The only thing to be worked out was how progressives and fundamentalists could get along in the same building. As the fundamentalist teacher put it, "My students are quiet and orderly and they won't disturb anybody. The other students are the ones who talk and move around so much. If you can find a way for your students not to disturb mine we'll get along fine." The compromise reached created more problems than it solved. The black community was relegated to an old school and the new school became increasingly fundamentalist. A third teacher was hired who was more fundamentalist than not. The two one-room schools were now four one-room schools, three physically attached and one separate. There was no unity of purpose or philosophy and the white parents could choose which of the three classes they preferred. Each class was multigraded, and each teacher had control of a small budget and, within limits created by the parents, the power to teach as he or she chose.

Elizabeth's child, Alice, hated school and schools. There was altogether too much talk about schools and education around her house. She liked to read, to run with the boys, and to be left alone. She couldn't understand why her mother worried so much about what was happening in the school. To her, school was a place you tolerated for five hours a day and also a place where you occasionally learned something interesting. It wasn't until she was fourteen, in 1871, that school seemed more than a chore to her. For Christmas in 1871 one of her uncles gave her a copy of Louisa May Alcott's *Little Men*. He knew she loved *Little Women* and felt close to the wild tomboyish Jo, and supposed correctly that Alice would like to know what happened to Jo when she grew up.

"Jo became a teacher, that's what!" Alice told her mother. At first Alice was disappointed, but as the book unfolded it became clear that Jo's school was not like her school. There was an understanding of child life that she hadn't experienced in Turin. And there was a mixing of classes and a compassionate understanding of children in trouble that she had never experienced. She identified with Nan, the tough, experienced girl, and fell in love with Nat and his fiddle. She also wanted to know about Louisa May Alcott the writer and asked her mother, who seemed to know or know about everybody.

Elizabeth laughed a bit at the question. She knew of the Alcotts, not just Louisa May but the whole family. She took down a book to show to Alice. It was Elizabeth Peabody's *Record of a School* published in 1835 in Boston. It was the story of the Temple School run by Bronson Alcott, Louisa May's father. Alice knew about Elizabeth Peabody, the kindergarten lady who had lectured in Turin. She was one of her mother's idols, the person responsible for introducing kindergartens into the United States and known for defending the rights and dignity of children.

Elizabeth explained to Alice that Bronson Alcott tried to create a school where boys and girls of all classes could go to school together and grow naturally and with love for each other in the world. He even took in a black student at a time when there were hardly any other integrated schools in the country. That was in the 1830s and people couldn't tolerate his ideas and principles. Also he was a little strange and dogmatic. For many reasons, the school didn't last long, but Bronson's daughter Louisa May made it live on in *Little Men*. Jo, the wild one of *Little Women*, became what in the 1860s and 1870s was called a "modern teacher." She believed in child-centered learning, in collective work with children, and in learning through experimentation. She advocated what Henry Barnard (later the first United States Commissioner of Education) described in 1868 as education, as opposed to instruction:

Instruction calls into exercise a sort of passive activity, a reception of facts and a perception of relations as presented. Education trains the pupil to discover relationships, and to make deductions from facts, and thus excites independent activity. Teachers and books instruct when they convey thoughts and explain processes; they educate in so far as they lead the pupil or reader to think for himself and to institute new processes. . . . Thus although instruction and education are inseparable, there may be much instruction where there is very little education, and very little instruction where there is much education. *Instruction is limited to what the teacher does; education is measured by what the pupil is rendered competent to perform.*[12]

As Alice got older she overcame her reluctance to imitate her mother and toyed with the idea of teaching. When she was eighteen, her mother, who was usually not so aggressive, gave her a book called *Reminiscences of Friedrich Froebel*, written by Baroness von Marenholz-Bulow and translated into English by Mary Mann, the second wife of Horace Mann and sister of Elizabeth Peabody. The book told of the baroness's relations with Froebel and described the magic of his kindergartens. Alice was particularly moved when Froebel was quoted as saying, "The kindergarten is the free republic of childhood." She remembered her mother's favorite quote from *Uncle Tom's Cabin:* "The child is the only true democrat." She found herself caught up in the romance of education. She volunteered to help out in the schools at Turin and after a while decided she could be more useful tutoring reading at the school in the black community than at the one she attended.

Elizabeth, despite her age, kept up on things happening in education. She followed the work of Henry Barnard, subscribed to all the journals of modern education, and kept a correspondence with dozens of educators throughout the country. She contributed to many journals, though no one in Turin, including her own daughter, would have suspected that she was highly regarded as an educational thinker. One experiment that she followed with particular interest took place in Quincy, Massachusetts, in 1873.

> The school board of Quincy, Massachusetts, sensing that all was not right with the system, decided to conduct the annual school examinations in person. The results were disastrous. While the youngsters knew their rules of grammar thoroughly, they could not write an ordinary English letter. While they could read with facility from their textbooks, they were utterly confused by similar material from unfamiliar sources. And while they spelled speedily through the required word lists, the orthography of their letters was atrocious. The board left determined to make some changes, and after a canvass of likely candidates, elected Francis Wayland Parker as superintendent.[13]

Parker, known to everyone as Colonel Parker since his service in the Civil War, was a schoolteacher before the war. He began teaching in 1853 at the age of sixteen and worked with young people until the Civil War. After the war he taught in Dayton, Ohio, where he was the principal of the first normal training school (as teacher-training institutes were called) in the city. He got in trouble in Dayton for criticizing textbooks. He was attacked by the publishing companies, but he was a tough fighter and emerged as assistant superintendent in Dayton. In 1871, after his wife died unexpectedly, Parker left Dayton bereaved. Instead of going back to teaching, he went to Europe, following the same path as Calvin Stowe, Horace Mann, Henry Barnard, and other leading American educators. He met with Froebelians, visited Pestalozzi's school, and talked with educators throughout the continent. Upon returning to the United States he was hired by the Quincy, Massachusetts, school board.

In Quincy, Colonel Parker made drastic changes:

> The set curriculum was abandoned, and with it the speller, the reader, the grammar, and the copybook. Children were

started on simple words and sentences, rather than the alphabet learned by rote. In place of time-honored texts, magazines, newspapers, and materials devised by the teachers themselves were introduced into the classroom. Arithmetic was approached inductively, through objects rather than rules, while geography began with a series of trips over the local countryside. Drawing was added to encourage manual dexterity and individual expression. The emphasis throughout was on observing, describing, and understanding, and only when these abilities had begun to manifest themselves — among the faculty as well as the students — were more conventional studies introduced.

The program was an immediate success and attracted national attention as the "Quincy System." Teachers, school superintendents, and newspapermen descended on the schools in such numbers as to require restrictions to prevent interference with the daily work. . . . Parker himself decried the fuss, protesting that there was nothing at all novel about the Quincy approach. "I repeat," he wrote in his report of 1879, "that I am simply trying to apply well established principles of teaching, principles derived directly from the laws of the mind. The methods springing from them are found in the development of every child. They are used everywhere except in school. I have introduced no new principle, method, or detail. No experiments have been tried, and there is no peculiar 'Quincy System.' "[14]

Elizabeth was intrigued by Colonel Parker's work and felt that Parker's description of himself described her feelings about her own life and work perfectly:

I can say that all my life I have had a perfect passion for teaching school, never wavered in it in my life, and never desired to change. I never had anything outside offered me that had any real attraction for me, and I never decided to go outside the field — it was a sort of wonder to me that I did have such a love for it. I remember when I was teaching in the Grammar School in Piscataquog I had a small garden. Then we lived near the old home where I was born, and I had a bit of rocky, gravelly garden, that I used to tend and hoe, morning and night; beans and corn and so on. Always it seems to me when I was hoeing I was dreaming and thinking of school. I remember one day I was hoeing beans. I remember just where I stood when I said to myself, "Why do I love to teach school?" And then I looked around on the growing plants and said, "It is because I love to see things grow." If I should tell the secret of my life, it is the intense desire I have to see growth and improvement in all living things, and most of all human beings.[15]

Elizabeth read that quote often and dreamed of knowing more about how Parker and his coworkers did what she had been trying to do for years. Colonel Parker left Quincy in 1882 to become director of the Cook County Normal School in Chicago, to work with children and to train teachers. If only Alice were interested in becoming a teacher!

Alice had enough of the volunteer life. She was considering marriage, considering going to normal school, considering many things since she passed twenty-five. When Elizabeth finally got the courage to tell Alice about the Cook County Normal School and the possibility of going to Chicago to study, Alice was ready. Chicago was a solution of sorts. It would give her two years to think and learn, to decide whether she wanted to stay in Turin to have a family, or teach, or both, since it was now possible. Alice had no problem getting into the Cook County Normal School and arrived in Chicago in the fall of 1883. Several letters she wrote to her fiancé, Ralph Burns, described her impressions:

Chicago, October 15, 1883

My Dear Ralph,

Your letter reached me a few days ago. I want to thank you for its great and kind support for my current adventure. Chicago is not a kind place for one used to the size and dimension of life in Turin. Without the kind assistance of Pastor Bennor and the generosity of the congregation, I would have abandoned this city and returned to my small and comfortable classroom.

Please give my warmest regards to your family and my parents, who should have received several letters during the last week. Give my special regards to my mother and inform her that in the next week I will have an interview with Colonel Parker. I am not sure whether to thank her for convincing me to travel so far from Turin or to beg her for permission to give up and return home.

Please think well of me. Yours faithfully and with warmest regards,

Alice

Chicago, October 29, 1883

My Dear Ralph,

It has been most encouraging having your letters come so often and so regularly. My interview with Colonel Parker has finally arrived and passed. I am very confused by what I have seen and what he has said and done.

Colonel Parker is a large man though it is genuinely difficult to gauge the size of him. He doesn't sit down and doesn't do just one thing at a time. During my brief interview, there were children coming to him with questions about every subject. There were visitors from New York, a journalist who had come to inspect the school, and several teachers undergoing training. I don't know if I can be at all like them and don't know how I'll manage the constant activity around here.

I simply do not understand what is happening at the school. Rose Thomas, one of the teachers, gave me a tour, but I cannot say what I have seen. Forgive my confusion. I must write to mother and ask her what to expect.

Your warm and confused friend,

Alice

Chicago, December 1, 1883

Dearest Ralph,

I do not know what is more remarkable, the public school or the course of study at the Cook County Normal School.

*Colonel Parker said in a talk to new students that a course
of study must be flexible if he is to train flexible teachers. We
are all to do manual labor, to study the history of education,
and to learn how to teach reading and arithmetic without the
use of textbooks or workbooks. Colonel Parker said that textbooks are the work of the devil and they shrivel minds.*

*Today I was introduced to printing, which I am to master.
I have not seen a printing press before, much less used one.
But learning to operate a press is part of my instruction in
the teaching of reading. The press is used to print our reading lessons, which consist of our children's poems and stories
as well as the remarkable writings on scientific observations
they make in Mr. Jackman's class and upon class trips. The
press is also used to prepare material for the* Chicago Normal
School Envelope, *which is written by Colonel Parker and the
rest of the staff. The* Envelopes *contain stories of the work
at the school and I have learned much from them.*

*I am extremely busy these days and hope you will forgive
me for not writing as often as in my time of confusion and
loneliness. I still hold you in the same high regard and think
of you often.*

Your warm friend,
Alice

March 3, 1884

Dearest Ralph,

*I believe I have seen a pattern to all the movement and
activity here. The key to understanding Colonel Parker's
work is to see that the children think for themselves, have a
voice in what happens at the school, and, though they are
cooperative and considerate, do not sit still waiting to be
given an assignment. I have never been so tired working
with young people and never so elated.*

*I am working on a unit on employment and workers' or-
ganizations in Chicago. We have studied the crafts unions
and some cooperatives. I have talked with a representative
of the Knights of Labor who will visit the school. The class is
planning a pageant depicting the history of Working People
in America. The students in art are making posters and cos-*

tumes. My reading class is writing the script and we will print it at the school. The woodworking class is making a speaker's platform and models of factories. I have never seen so much bustle. A visitor would think us possessed and disorganized, yet it all coheres about a theme so that one of our young carpenters could tell of labor history and our actors know just what our carpenters are up to.

All this is the more astonishing in that Colonel Parker is under constant attack from the Chicago Tribune *and certain members of the Chicago school board. They simply do not or will not understand what we are doing. Occasionally I can see the Colonel's mustache twitch and imagine him to be trembling with rage. At times he walks the halls muttering "how long, how long," though he said at assembly yesterday, and we believe him, that someday people will understand our work for the children.*

I look forward to resting and spending the summer being with you in Turin. Please share this with mother as I have no time to write. The Colonel insisted that I contribute my unit to the Envelope, *and though I protested my inadequacy, he said that if one's work is too poor to bear the light of day, it is too poor to occupy the time of children. And seeing my hesitancy he added that the greatest courage is to make mistakes and grow through them. I don't know but that I might become a writer too.*

With warmest regards I remain your friend,

Alice

Alice returned to Turin the summer of 1884 and finished her training at the Cook County Normal School the next year. In the summer of 1885 she married Ralph Burns. She was also fortunate enough to get a job at the Turin Common School, which kept on growing as Turin and the United States became industrialized. Alice's work was accepted. A modern America entering the twentieth century would need modern schools that stressed flexibility, invention, and the ability to adjust to the social demands of progress. The newspapers during the '90s called the twentieth century The

Century of the Child; it was also called the American Century.

Progressives grew as industry grew. In Turin, attacks were mounted on fundamentalist education from two groups, both in the name of progress. One group felt that it was basic that school prepare students to take their roles in a growing industrial world. The other group agreed that students should be prepared for industrial society, but it added to that preparation for a socially progressive society. The former group consisted of many members of the business and farming community as well as managers of the steel mill and the tool-and-die factory that had just opened outside of town. The latter consisted of some farmers, workers, and business people, who ranged from Teddy Roosevelt Progressives to Eugene Debs socialists. Both groups agreed that fundamentalist education was inadequate for the twentieth century.

As one of the members of the Chamber of Commerce put it, "Children have to be prepared for change. Reading, writing, and arithmetic won't be enough in the new century. They must learn how to learn."

In that context Joseph Mayer Rice's indictment of the public schools published in 1893 was widely read and discussed.[16]

People were also concerned a few years later with Scott Nearing's analysis of the effects of a rigid minimal three-Rs curriculum:

It is probable that the majority of children who enter American schools receive no more education than will enable them to read clumsily, to write badly, to spell wretchedly, and to do the simplest math problem (add, subtract, etc.) with difficulty. In any real sense of the word, they are neither educated nor cultured.[17]

Alice discussed educational issues with her mother, Elizabeth, right up until Elizabeth passed away in 1894. They followed Joseph Mayer Rice's articles on the schools in *The Forum* and appreciated his defense of Colonel Parker. Yet Alice more than her mother sensed something lacking in "modern" education too. The late nineteenth century was substantially different from pre–Civil War America. Many of the older books seemed stiff and outmoded. The math and science taught even in the "modern" schools was obsolete. Children of the twentieth century would have to deal with new needs of society, with engineering and mechanization, with increased mobility. How could education be useful in an industrial society and still be natural and humane? That was a major question that Alice and many of her contemporaries struggled with.

In 1896, two years after her mother's death, Alice decided to return to Chicago for renewal. She had taken a leave from teaching in 1895 when her first child, Phillip, was born and wasn't sure whether she had the energy to return to the classroom. Her aunt took care of the baby, and Ralph somewhat reluctantly let her go. Her old friend and teacher from the normal school, Rose Thomas, had a large house and gave Alice a room. During the time of Alice's stay in Chicago from spring 1896 to spring 1897, the following events were held at the University of Chicago campus: the annual institute of the Cook County Teachers; a meeting of the Illinois Society for Child Study; conferences on teaching English, mathematics, reading, the arts; a celebration of Horace Mann's Centennial; a celebration of the 150th anniversary of the birth of Pestalozzi; and most important for Alice, a series of public lectures on the science and art of teaching by Colonel Parker, and a seminar on education conducted by Professor John Dewey, who had arrived in Chicago in 1894.[18] Alice heard of Dewey from Rose, who first met him when he enrolled his children in Colonel Parker's school. Rose also attended Dewey's first seminar on education at the University of Chicago.

Colonel Parker's lectures were Alice's main source of renewal. His theory of concentration, which put the natural and human sciences at the center of the curriculum, even for the very young, confirmed what Alice had learned from her own work with children. Language and math skills grew out of studying what was interesting. You didn't first teach discrete reading and math skills and then hope they would be applied. You began with a lively exploration of the world and made it clear to children how reading and number skills enriched that exploration. Colonel Parker's diagram of his theory became for Alice what the framed quote from Froebel was for her mother. She framed it and put it over the study desk she built for herself in her living room. (See chart on p. 55.)

Alice realized in Chicago that she wanted to return to the classroom. Hearing about Pestalozzi and Horace Mann, celebrating their work, made her think of her mother's work and all the unfinished tasks in Turin, the deprived black children, the children of factory workers, the East European immigrant children who were arriving in greater numbers. There were old unsolved school problems and new ones resulting from immigration and industrial growth. Professor Dewey tried to address himself to these problems and to the philosophical base for educational action as well.

Dewey was in many ways the opposite of Colonel Parker. He was dry and a bit wry, given to rambling. Someone in his seminar said that he spoke the longest paragraphs in the world. However, his students recognized that, however involuted and complex his words were, they had weight and substance. Dewey in his early work tried to reconcile the free individual, the natural person, with the citizen in an industrial state. How can children be educated so that industry and progress serve the growth of all the people rather than merely profit a few? That was Dewey's challenge, and in 1897, toward the end of Alice's stay in Chicago, Dewey published *My Pedagogic Creed,* which became as important to Alice as *Uncle Tom's Cabin* was to her mother.

Upon returning to Turin, Alice shared Dewey's work with

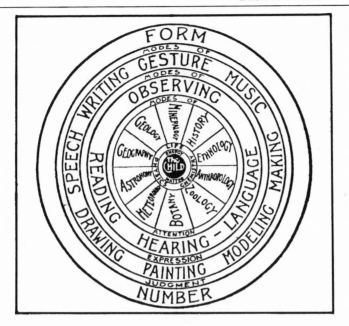

her friends and colleagues. She was particularly taken with the end of the *Pedagogic Creed,* where Dewey stated,

> I believe that education is a regulation of the process of coming to share in the social consciousness; and that the adjustment of individual activity on the basis of this social consciousness is the only sure method of social reconstruction.
> I believe that this conception has due regard for both the individualistic and socialistic ideals.[19]

"Due regard for both the individualistic and socialistic ideals." That was what Alice's goal in the classroom had been, was the legacy her mother had left her. Alice remembered the project she'd done at the normal school on working people in America and planned a whole series of projects for her return to teaching. She would use Colonel Parker's idea of putting content at the core of the curriculum, but her content would be social, not geological or geographic. Ralph warned her that she might be asking for trouble. He wasn't so sure this Dewey wasn't a red, and besides, he didn't like Alice's partiality to Eugene Debs in politics. Alice went ahead, as did hundreds of other teachers, in developing the social content of the curriculum.

Her class of sixth graders explored their community. (During the time of her absence, the school had reached a critical mass, and it had been decided to imitate some of the larger cities and group students by age, which was considered quite progressive at the time.) The students did voter surveys, talked to people in local businesses and in the factories. They visited poor families, and spoke with a few pioneer social workers (friends of Alice's from Chicago, where they were trained by Jane Addams at Hull House). They wrote about what improvements were needed in the community, and became involved in a project to build a park in the immigrant section of town. They also read books about the kinds of things they were experiencing. Some of the parents didn't approve of Alice's methods and there was some grumbling. Because of the reorganization of the school, everyone had to have their twelve-year-olds in Alice's class and conflict was bound to develop. When parental choice was taken away by the school board, parental conflict increased. Alice was able to survive the grumbling and occasional hostility because no parents could ever say that their children didn't learn reading, spelling, and arithmetic. She practiced what she learned from Colonel Parker, that openness does not mean an abandonment of standards.

At the turn of the century Alice was a Deweyite, a socialist who did not believe in violent revolution but who did believe, as Dewey put it, that

> it is fatal for a democracy to permit the formation of fixed classes. Differences of wealth, the existence of large masses of unskilled laborers, contempt for work with the hands, inability to secure the training which enables one to forge ahead in life, all operate to produce classes and to widen the gulf between them.[20]

Not everybody who believed in progress and industrialization believed that schools should train students to create a socialist society. Many people in Turin who agreed with certain aspects of Dewey's pedagogic ideas disagreed with his social goals. One could believe in training students to think, in learning through doing and through involvement in community activities, in preparing students to respond to the varying and often unpredictable demands of a growing industrial society and international power, and still be a capitalist.

The people in Turin who were not Dewey socialists and yet wanted to modernize the schools called their plans for the school the Bessemer model of education. This model developed by analogy with the Bessemer process for making steel. Before Bessemer developed this process, steel was made by heating iron ore very carefully in order to eliminate impurities and at the same time keep in the right amount of carbon needed to produce a good grade of steel. This process required great skill and was quite unreliable. Bessemer developed a completely different way of making steel. The Bessemer process consisted of superheating the iron ore to drive out all of the carbon and other impurities and then to add back to the melted-down ore just the right quantities of carbon and other substances needed to make high-quality steel. It was a simpler, more efficient and predictable process.

The Bessemer process of education advocated by a number of people in Turin and other places throughout the country was to get rid of everything that didn't work in the schools and if possible begin all over again in a scientific way. Techniques, materials, and people were to be brought into school under scrutiny. Everything should be studied, and whatever didn't work should be eliminated. It was hoped that through this process schools would produce high-quality students just as the Bessemer process produced high-grade steel.

About this time, in the first decades of the twentieth century, the "science of education" was developing. I.Q. and achievement tests were being tried out for the first time on a fairly large scale. A number of educators at teacher training institutions (many of which were now colleges instead of normal schools) became involved in planning programs for local school districts. Often these educators (many of whom considered themselves scientific progressives) were not schoolteachers but trained psychologists and statisticians. They believed that the schools, especially in large districts, needed rational planning and scientific management. Many of the plans they made laid the groundwork for the development of nonteaching school bureaucracies.

In 1904, at the request of the local business community, the school board in Turin turned to the state teachers college for advice. A professor from the state university in Canton visited Turin and studied the situation, and recommended that the district hire a professional principal/superintendent, a trained educational expert, who could develop a unified program for the community and train teachers in current methods. He also recommended that the school for black students be closed, that Alice's school be enlarged, and that the children in the expanded plant be grouped by ability, with two classes on each grade. That way, he implied in his report to the school board, blacks and immigrants could be separated from "native" children on a scientific basis.

Alice and her colleagues resented the new plans as did many members of the community. The experts hadn't consulted them. A plan was drawn up without any local input, the gist of which was to put an outside expert in charge of the whole system. The teachers felt that, even though they had differing educational and political views, they had evolved ways of living together and making communal decisions about issues that affected the whole school. Now their power was taken away in the name of science and they had no idea what would be imposed upon them. Alice, as chosen representative of the staff, spoke before a board meeting opposing the experts' recommendations. However, the business community's representatives were adamant that scientific planning was needed if schools were to serve changing social and economic conditions. The recommendations were accepted with the specific promise, insisted upon by the fundamentalists and the business community, that an Americanization program be instituted as soon as the new principal/superintendent took over.

Americanization was a major issue in the schools in the early twentieth century. In Turin the new mill and factory attracted workers who had recently come from Italy and eastern Europe. This new influx of peoples created problems for schools throughout the country. The immigrants did not speak English and the teachers were not trained to work with students who couldn't understand them. The newcomers also had cultural habits that seemed strange to Turin's old-timers. They became "problems" and their children were "problems."

In New York City, for example, there were complaints about Irish and Italian students being unmanageable in the schools and lawless on the streets. Discipline and Americanization were thought to be solutions to these problems of ghetto schools. However, the students resisted. Angelo Patri, in his book *A Schoolmaster of the Great City,* described his first teaching experience in a public school in East Harlem in 1907. He was given fifty students and he tried to use the strict methods he was trained to use. He discovered that "discipline, my great stronghold, had failed for I had come into contact with those who defied discipline."[21]

Patri had heard his "fellow teachers . . . talking about Education, the Science of Education and its principles. It appeared that there were men who could teach a man why he taught and how to do it. There was one thing I had learned and that was the insufficiency of my equipment as a teacher. Discipline, boss standard, was nerve taxing and not altogether productive."[22]

Patri went to Teachers College, Columbia, in 1907, just a

few years after John Dewey had moved from the University
of Chicago to Columbia. After Columbia, Patri returned to
teaching with new principles and with a belief that

> unless a school enters deeply into the lives of the people, that
> school will not enter deeply into the lives of the children or
> into the lives of the teachers. Unless the school is the great
> democratic socializing agency, it is nothing at all.[23]

Patri put his progressive and scientific views on education
into practice upon returning to teaching and as principal of
a junior high created a model of a progressive urban immigrant ghetto school.

Alice was to meet Angelo Patri in 1920 when he was the
keynote speaker of the first meeting of the Progressive Education Association, which she joined as soon as she heard about
it in 1919, the year it was founded. Before that she was a
member of the National Educational Association, which she
joined in 1905 in order to keep in touch with developments
in her profession. The first twenty years of the century were
exciting ones in education. The work of Colonel Parker and
others, as well as the ideas of John Dewey, seemed to be
coming to fruition.

Alice was representative of this progressive movement
and brought that perspective to the superintendent selection
committee in Turin. Searching for an acceptable principal/
superintendent was harder than anticipated. One criterion
for selection that quickly emerged from community debate
was that the new administrator be able to deal with pressure
and conflict. No single idea about what the basic role of the
school should be was going to be accepted by all the citizens
of Turin.

Despite the problems, the job was filled in 1905. There
were many people coming out of teachers college with
energy and new ideas at the turn of the century. The new
superintendent was a kind of educator the community had
not experienced before. Because of the number of divisions

within the community, the board decided to choose someone who claimed to be neutral politically and scientific
educationally. They chose John Dorfman, a person who had
big city teaching experience, was a principal in a small city,
and had done several semesters of graduate work at Teachers
College, Columbia, with Edward Thorndike and his students,
on the measurement of teacher effectiveness and pupil
achievement.

Dorfman puzzled Alice. He considered himself an educational progressive and supported her work. At the same time,
he disassociated himself from progressive political ideas,
which to Alice were the basis of progressive educational
practice. He also worried her with his talk of testing and
science. Yet she admitted that he helped the school overcome many educational and social problems. Dorfman arrived with a family, and his three children were immediately
enrolled in the public schools. His wife became active in
local civic organizations, and Dorfman worked hard, usually
twelve hours a day, trying to reorganize and expand the
school. He appeased the Deweyites by integrating community learning and activity methods in the curriculum. He
quieted the fundamentalists by instituting achievement tests
to prove that reading, writing, and arithmetic were learned.
He persuaded the business community to raise a bond issue
in order to build a new modern wing for the school. He
seemed to incorporate all the different views in the community into the school, but there was a vague sense that by
incorporating everything, nothing of substance was happening. The teachers were afraid to say much for fear he
would find out about their internal conflicts. Alice was the
only one who spoke out and she got what she wanted for
her class. Parents weren't sure about what to object to. They
had no way to find out whether their children were learning
more or less. The school was progressive and it wasn't; people
were content and they weren't; and worrying about schooling became boring. For a while most people decided to leave

the school in the hands of the principal, the professional, and turn to other community matters.

The advent of a principal/superintendent who considered himself a "professional" interested in the "science of education" had some interesting effects on the school. The principal made educational decisions without consulting people in the community. The school board's function was restricted for a while to voting confidence in the administrator's decisions. One of the teachers left and a new teacher, whom the principal had worked with before, was hired. Soon after the new teacher came in, the principal proposed a major reorganization of the school into an upper and lower division.

In 1910, after almost six years in Turin, Dorfman presented his comprehensive plan for the school. The new wing of the school was almost finished and Dorfman felt secure enough to make his move. The boldness of the plan shocked even Alice. It was based on the Gary Model, which was a plan for the reorganization of the Gary, Indiana, public schools that was being put into effect by William Wert, the superintendent in Gary.

The Gary Plan was an attempt to translate many of John Dewey's ideas into practice in an urban industrialized community. The school was to become the center of social, artistic, and intellectual life in the community. It would be open all day every day of the year. This way it could provide adult education classes, especially English and citizenship classes, for the immigrant community. The school would also provide community services, have a nursery and health clinic, teach nutrition and vocational education. The school itself would be organized into four centers: the shops, the labs and classrooms, the auditorium, and the playground. Students would rotate from one center to another on what came to be known as "the platoon system" or what we now call departmentalized learning. Teachers would become specialists, and instead of building new classrooms every time the student body increased, the utilization of the gym and auditorium by half of the pupils at any one time would allow teaching to occur in a small number of classrooms. The program was designed to be progressive and economical.

Students would no longer have their own classrooms for the whole day but move from teacher to teacher. Instead of having their own desks, students would be given lockers in the hall. Perhaps the major lasting effects of the Gary Plan initiated in 1907 were these lockers and the departmental system, which now symbolize, ironically enough, dehumanizing aspects of school life.

When John Dorfman presented his version of the Gary Plan to the school board in Turin, everyone was shocked. Some people called it socialistic; others called it downright foolish. However, two aspects of the plan did make sense to the school board. One was the departmental system, which would save the school from building new classrooms even if the student population grew. The other was adult classes in English and citizenship. The board instructed Dorfman to proceed with those aspects of his plan and in private they told him to forget about those notions of the school as a social and community center.

The teachers resisted the reorganization. They didn't want to become specialists, were afraid they didn't have the knowledge, didn't want to teach five classes a day in one subject instead of one class in all subjects. They also felt that so much moving around from place to place would not be any good for the younger children. Alice was tempted by the program as she had wanted, for some time, to concentrate on developing some projects in writing and social studies. However, she too was cynical about such a drastic reorganization of the school. After many heated battles at faculty meetings, it was decided that the plan would be modified so that the upper division would adopt the platoon system and the lower division would remain in single classrooms. The cutoff between the divisions would be for twelve-year-olds or sixth graders, who would be the oldest children to remain in self-contained classrooms.

Alice volunteered to be an English–Social Studies teacher

under the condition that the school board send her to a training institute so that she could prepare herself for this new role. The principal and board agreed and she spent the summer of 1911 at Teachers College, Columbia. As she told her family, it was good to have a new challenge when you were over fifty.

At Columbia she attended a seminar with Professor Dewey once again and took a class on curriculum-making with Professor William Hurd Kilpatrick. In that class Kilpatrick talked about the project method of organizing curriculum, too much as if he invented, Alice thought, remembering her work at the Cook County Normal School. Nevertheless, she had to admit that Professor Kilpatrick had thought through ways to organize projects and that his ideas would be useful to her when she returned. She summarized her ideas of how a project developed and kept them pinned over the desk of her study at home:

> Projects arise from (1) A desire to understand the meaning and use of some fact, phenomenon, or experience. This leads to questions and problems. (2) A conviction that it is worthwhile and possible to secure an understanding of the thing in question. This causes one to work with an impelling interest. (3) The gathering from experience, books, and experiments of the needed information, and the application of this information to answer the question in hand.[24]

Alice always felt that the years from 1911 to 1917 were the most creative of her teaching career. She realized that there was some grumbling that the school's reorganization was reducing standards. But, her teaching kept her alive. The reorganization put her in contact with immigrant and black children more fully than she had ever been. She was appalled at how badly taught these children had been before they came to her and resolved to compensate for their educational neglect. During those years she thought about her mother a lot, and realized how close their commitment and work was even though it manifested itself in different forms.

World War I was a terrible experience for the people in Turin as for the rest of the nation. There were two military drafts, a white draft and a colored draft, and the segregation that existed in the services during the war broke down the fragile bonds that were developing between the black and white communities. There were fights between the German immigrant community and the Anglo-Saxon community. People often took sides on the basis of national origin, and Alice saw all this in the schools, children fighting or refusing to associate with other groups of children. And the Russian Revolution led to a larger scale of red fear and red hating than she had experienced. People treated her with suspicion, as she had been a member of the Socialist party. During the last years of her teaching career, from 1919 to 1925, Alice spent most of her time trying to heal the old wounds the war exacerbated. She also became more active in the National Education Association and the Progressive Education Association. In 1921, when the NEA created a delegate assembly, Alice became an Ohio delegate and in 1923, at the annual meeting of the delegate assembly, which was held in Oakland, California, Alice presented a paper on how to use the project method to help students deal with cultural and racial differences.

At that meeting Alice heard several things that distressed her and reminded her how far we were from achieving her mother's goal of excellent schools for all the children of all of the people. She didn't consider herself much of a radical but worried that sensible progressive change would be crushed by purges within the education profession. She knew she was one of the anarchists being referred to in the address by James Fisk, chairman of the Americanism Commission of the American Legion who warned the delegates about anarchists, socialists, and all other progressives.

Alice found the talk by Ellwood Cubberly, Dean of the School of Education of Stanford University, to be particularly interesting. He articulated the problems she had been experiencing and came up with a program she thought was somewhat helpful:

> The six most important items in any forward-looking American school program, covering at least the next decade of work and service, are: (1) A comprehensive educational program to aid in the assimilation of the foreign-born we have among us; (2) the general provision of a good system of health and development education; (3) such a reorganization of our school curricula as will adapt our school better to new conditions and needs in our National life; (4) the reorganization and redirection of rural education; (5) a much more general equalization of both the advantages and the burdens of education than we now enjoy; and (6) provision for the placing of an adequately educated and an adequately trained teacher in every classroom in the United States. Five of these six are at bottom economic problems in that the necessary additional funds must be provided by our people before much can be done by educational workers to give effect to the proposals; only one — that of curricula reorganization — is primarily an educational problem. All of the six are primarily National in scope and importance, and call for National cooperation in their solution. In closing, let me add one more, and one which may easily become the major problem of them all.[25]

That last problem, which underlined the rest, was the absence of strong federal funding for education. The main theme of the convention in 1923 and over the next decade was the need for a strong Department of Education to equalize state funding for education so that poor states would be able to spend as much on schools as rich states, and to provide funds for educational research.

Alice had mixed feelings about these issues. In Ohio there was a strong tradition of local control of schools and Turin was no exception. Alice worried about whether Turin could solve its unique problems if there was strong federal control.

Alice was even more distressed by what she saw as an increasing dominance of the National Education Association by university-based researchers. She had to exert considerable self-control throughout the speech by Charles Judd, who was the current director of the School of Education at the University of Chicago, Colonel Parker rest in peace. She made notes of his remarks, quoting them whenever she talked to classroom teachers and tried to remind them of the importance of using classroom knowledge, rather than bowing to demands imposed by "experts" who knew nothing about teaching. Her favorite quote was:

> *My plea to this Association is that it make itself the center for the promotion of the one type of control that can find a permanent home on this continent — namely, control through research.*[26]

After reading this last quote Alice would tell the teachers that what she had learned in her career was that educational problems were, at bottom, not academic research questions, but issues of the heart and the will. That was the problem with her principal, John Dorfman, and with other administrators. They had research solutions that usually didn't work since they ignored the social and human context of learning.

Alice retired in 1925 and her two children didn't follow her into teaching. Her son Phillip became a dentist. He remained in Turin, taking a layman's interest in the schools, and during the thirties became a school board member. Her daughter, Elizabeth Ann, went to the University of Chicago School of Education at her mother's suggestion but transferred into the Department of Sociology. After college she moved to New York and received an M.A. in social work from Columbia. She remained in New York, working at the Henry Street Settlement House.

The main educational issue in Turin after the First World War was consolidation. The town was growing. It annexed two small unincorporated townships on its borders, and with that, the size of the school district almost doubled.

John Dorfman led the fight to build a new comprehensive

high school and to turn the Turin school and the two schools from the newly annexed town into elementary schools. The fight for consolidation was supported by a coalition of business people, progressives, and labor leaders who were trying to organize some of the local workers. They believed the high school would provide a better opportunity for students to acquire the range of skills needed to deal with the modern world. A science lab, special math and English teachers, an athletic program, a machine shop, and printing program all seemed possible with consolidation.

Opposition to consolidation came from people who feared loss of local control. They argued that a big district would put the power of taxation out of their hands. It would make it harder for the school to be accountable to the various segments of the community. It would lead to a deterioration in basic skills and a general lowering of standards. Dorfman countered this argument by showing people a battery of newly developed achievement tests. He explained how the use of tests during the war had led to the refinement of the science of testing and assured the community that, with the use of an extensive testing program, students' progress could be monitored and standards maintained. None of the school board members or community leaders knew much about this new science of education, but accepted on faith that science made as dramatic a contribution to education as it did to technology and business. Consolidation passed and John Dorfman became the first superintendent of the Turin Unified School District.

The new principal of the common school (now called the Turin Grammar School) was chosen by the superintendent and the enlarged unified school district. There was considerable grumbling in town about outsiders choosing their principal and rumors about him being a Communist and having a perverted sex life. The Russian Revolution and bohemian life in Greenwich Village were in the news those days and there were constant allusions to progressives being

Communists or libertines. Of course, there were socialist progressive educators, child-centered progressives, and scientific progressives like the former principal/superintendent. There were probably some progressives who were Communists and some who had complicated sex lives. However, the progressive-education movement was not unified, though through John Dewey's name and the leadership he provided, it gave the impression of unity from without. From within, progressives battled other progressives, sometimes with greater energy than they expended in putting their ideas into practice.

The new principal in Turin was neither Communist nor libertarian. He was an energetic man in his late fifties who loved working with students. He is remembered by old-timers these days as a wonderful man who created an administrative mess. The principal's interest was in the "project method," and he worked with the teachers and older students to develop a project curriculum for the whole school. He even persuaded Alice to come out of retirement and train the teachers in the project method. Alice and Walter Johnson became close friends and worked together until Alice died of emphysema in 1933.

The curriculum at the Turin Grammar School was reorganized so that subject areas were replaced by projects, an idea John Dorfman supported but couldn't effect when he was principal. Now that he was superintendent he could provide the support for Walter Johnson to do it and he even made Alice part-time curriculum supervisor.

Each project was meant to relate to life in the community and to subjects that interested the students. The projects were to integrate reading, writing, math, science, the arts, and social studies. They were not to be chosen at random but in such a way that the skills students had to learn would be carefully integrated into project study. In getting approval to develop a project curriculum for the Turin Grammar School and help the other grammar schools develop project curricula as well, Dorfman had the following quote entered into the school board's resolution approving the project as the basic component of the school program:

> If the project is to be made the basis of the curriculum, it is necessary for the teacher to decide as scientifically as possible what principles and processes should be mastered by the student and then to select not single projects but projects so arranged that selection of projects is made possible with the certainty that all essential facts, processes, and principles will be covered.[27]

Some of the projects students studied in Turin were:

EARLY GRADES (K TO 1, 2)

1. planning, building, and planting a student-run vegetable garden;
2. studying the post office and setting up a student post office in the school;
3. studying and visiting the steel mill and the tool-and-die factory;
4. studying health and visiting and helping the town doctor and nurse.

UPPER GRADES (3 TO 6)

1. collecting stamps and doing research on the places the stamps came from;
2. studying machinery and building a small electric go-cart;
3. from ranch to table: studying the flow of food from growing and raising to processing and marketing, visiting wholesalers, ranchers, farmers, and retail stores.

These projects represent just a few of those developed in Turin and throughout the country. The ultimate goal was to articulate them into a comprehensive curriculum over the years.

There were parents and teachers in Turin who were angry at having the project method forced into the school. They felt it represented a neglect of the three Rs and they didn't trust the test results produced by the superintendent to support his claim that skills were mastered best through developing interesting content. They were also angry about questions children were dealing with in school. There was no place, they claimed, for students raising social issues or questioning authority in the schools. Many teachers resisted all of Dorfman's innovations and they had strong community support.

The depression hit Turin in the middle of the project method. There were major catastrophes in town. Money for the school was cut, some teachers had to leave. There was temporary panic and resentment from the more conservative members of the community. All these modern methods were worthless in a world of no jobs. The school should stick to reading, writing, and arithmetic, should not try to do so much. A new school board put pressure on the superintendent to cut programs, to eliminate anything that could be considered a frill. The principal's response was that his program was basic, that he didn't allow frills in his district. There were endless debates in barbershops, factories, and kitchens about what was basic in the society. The situation worsened until, in 1932, Roosevelt was elected with a mandate to give people a New Deal, to change society so all the people would have a good deal. There was grumbling among some people about socialism and communism, about loss of community control and federal interference in local affairs and business. But most people felt hope and believed that through planning, another 1929 could be avoided. The high school worked with the CCC; the grammar schools in the district continued to develop projects with increasingly social content. "How can we help the community?" was a theme worked into many of the projects. Helping out was basic. All the skills were taught in order to help rebuild the society.

Ever since he had been appointed principal of the Turin Grammar School, Walter Johnson had been vowing to spend part of his day teaching his favorite subject, American History. Alice kidded him about that dream. She told him that he'd never get around to teaching again. He took it in a good-natured way but it depressed him. He loved to teach, and being a principal, though it had rewards, had none of the excitement of teaching for him. A few years after Alice died he decided to teach history to the upper grade of his school, "for Alice," as he said to his staff. He requested and got approval to buy a new social studies curriculum developed by Harold Rugg entitled *Man and His Changing Society,* and tested the curriculum in the schools himself. The curriculum was designed to assist students in thinking about different social systems, in analyzing social problems and considering alternate ways of solving them. At that time thousands of sets of the books were being used throughout the country.

Rugg's books tried to look at history from the perspective of working people. They tried to analyze problems associated with developing democracy in the United States. For example, in dealing with the making of the Constitution, Rugg analyzed the class and interests of the members of the Constitutional Convention and summarized the making of the United States Constitution in this way:

THE CONVENTION SET UP A GOVERNMENT BY WHICH CHANGES WERE MADE DIFFICULT

The Fathers of the Constitution feared "too much democracy." They were afraid of what the majority of people, who did not possess property, would do to the minority, who did. They were afraid of what they regarded as the ignorance and rashness of the lower classes.

The spoken and written words of the men in the Convention show very clearly that they regarded democracy as a dangerous thing. Gerry, for example, said that the unsettled condition of the country "came from the excess of democracy."

Randolph used almost the same words, pointing out that the bad times were due to "the turbulence and follies of democracy." Another delegate, during the debate over the qualifications for Senator, maintained that the Senate should be made up of wealthy men "to keep down the turbulence of democracy."

Even Madison wanted to protect the small class of well-to-do people against the majority, that is, against the common people. In one of his writings he said:

> "It is of great importance in a Republic not only to guard the society against the oppression of its rulers, but to guard one part of society against the injustice of the other part. Different interests necessarily exist in different classes of citizens. If a majority be united by a common interest the rights of the minority will be insecure."

Alexander Hamilton wanted Senators to serve for life. He said:

> "All communities divide themselves into the few and the many. The first are the rich and the well-born, the other, the mass of the people . . . are turbulent and changing; they seldom judge or determine right. Give, therefore, to the first class a distinct permanent share in the government. They will check the unsteadiness of the second, and as they cannot receive any advantage by change, they, therefore, will ever maintain good government."

Thus it was that the Fathers wished to guard against the dangers of too much democracy. How did they do it?[28]

The Rugg texts were accompanied by workbooks encouraging students to study their own community and to analyze current political and social events for themselves. The texts were published in the context of the Depression, where raising issues about the quality and purpose of the United States was natural. How could a society with such hope collapse so suddenly? And was the collapse sudden, or just the culmination of a long process of growth and the accumulation of wealth without regard for all of the people or for the creation of a sensible, self-renewing future?

These arguments focused on the schools in 1940 when the National Association of Manufacturers announced that it would investigate school textbooks that were supporting communism and undermining the American way of life. The NAM joined the American Legion and a coalition of conservative organizations called the American Coalition. They claimed that the specter of collectivism was sneaking into the schools and that they had to be "sentinels" to protect capitalist America. The target these groups selected for their most violent attacks were the Rugg textbooks, which raised questions about social systems but meticulously avoided telling students what to think. In September 1940, the *American Legion Magazine* published an article entitled "Treason in the Textbooks" by O. K. Armstrong, which contained a strong attack on the Rugg textbooks.

Turin was not immune from the attacks on Rugg's texts. The county office of the American Legion as well as some business organizations banded together to eliminate, not merely the textbooks, but Walter Johnson as well, from the Turin school. Walter defended his use of the books and cited a study by leading historians from Harvard and Dartmouth that affirmed that the texts did not distort the primary documents of United States history in any way. He had depended upon this study to quiet this opposition but it worked no better than the study of Colonel Parker's school did fifty years before. The opposition was political, not "scientific." The battle was won in the name of patriotism, fundamentalism, and, as one school board member said, "back to the basics." Walter Johnson resigned in early 1941. His resignation was accepted by the school board with only one dissenting vote, that of Dr. Phillip Burns, Alice's son.

Reaction to Walter Johnson's resignation was blunted by the onset of World War II, and for five years education went into the deep freeze. After the war the school grew at a phenomenal rate. Turin Grammar School doubled in size to about 300 students. The high school was up to 1500 by 1950. Educationally, things were mixed. There was still some project teaching going on. A few classes were run by teachers of the fundamentalist persuasion. There were some teachers who "taught by the book," meaning the teachers manual and the curriculum guides that came from the state board of education. The reading programs in the primary grades were indicative of the dispirited condition of the school. There was one teacher who taught strict phonics and swore by the book *Why Johnny Can't Read*. There was another one who taught by the look-and-see method and still used project learning. A third primary teacher used basal readers and workbooks. They never talked to each other about children or learning, and managed to get along without overt disagreement. The latest principal considered himself a manager, not an educator. Each teacher could do what he or she wanted as long as there was no trouble. The problem wasn't education so much as space and numbers.

The principal also knew what had happened in Pasadena in 1951, where the school board, using tactics similar to those that chased the Rugg text and the former superintendent out of Turin in the forties, ousted all the progressives in the district, from the superintendent on down. Anyone's job could be threatened during that time when innovation, progressivism, and communism were swept into one category.

During the early 1950s the principal's job was to keep things quiet and not let the unpleasantness associated with the departure of the former principal reoccur. The new man managed well and was supported by a large new middle class that developed during the postwar economic boom. They wanted an efficient school that would pass students on so they could eventually get into the newly expanded state college system.

Concern about the nature and quality of education became a national issue again only after the Russians launched *Sputnik* in 1957, and there was a great outcry that our schools were the reason we had fallen behind in science and technology. The effect of *Sputnik* was to focus educational concern on the development of excellence, particularly in the areas of science and technology. For many people in power, the basic task of public education shifted from providing education for all children to the creation of a technocratic elite that would make us competitive with Russia. Hard thinking, learning to deal with abstractions, and technical training became skills that were considered basic to the survival of our society. Ironically, many of these skills were precisely those advocated by the progressives during the '20s and '30s.

The boredom and uniformity of school as well as the lowering of standards associated with the life-adjustment philosophy current at the time were considered the culprits. The adjustment philosophy was the result of an enormous growth in the use of psychology in education. Psychologists in the schools were concerned with how students felt, with family problems, and with how students adapted to the social world of the school. They didn't worry much about math, science, reading — the so-called hard skills. The psychologists also pried into personal matters too much for the taste of some parents. The presumed lowering of standards and invasion of privacy caused by the adjustment philosophy led many parents in the late '50s to reluctantly enroll their children in private schools.

This reluctance was expressed by John Keats, a professional writer and critic of the schools, who explained why he took his own children out of the public schools and put them in an expensive and, according to him, excellent private school during the late 1950s:

> We think continually of those whom we have left behind;
> . . . of children whose potentialities will never be realized
> by a school system which puts conformity ahead of accom-

plishment, which substitutes techniques for understanding, which underestimates children's desire and ability to do hard mental work and which . . . defrauds our youth of their right to a decent education while pretending to adjust them to life.[29]

One of the students left behind in the public schools was Ralph Stokes Burns, son of Phillip Burns, grandson of Alice Burns, and great grandson of Elizabeth Stokes. The Burnses refused to abandon the public school even in the negative climate of the 1950s. They explained the importance of public education as best they could to their children, and were delighted when a few years later the new President, John F. Kennedy, was able to get the Elementary and Secondary Education Act passed. After some dry years, the new President whom the Burnses enthusiastically supported, managed to get the federal government to reaffirm support of the common schools. As part of this support, as well as in response to *Sputnik,* Kennedy also established an Office of Science and Technology at the Executive Office of the White House. That office convened a series of meetings of physicists, mathematicians, biologists, chemists, and other scientists, and set them to work on what later became the New Math, the New Biology, the New Physics. These curricula used many "learning by doing" principles, and had many hands-on activities. But what chiefly characterized them was a systematic approach to science based on current scientific knowledge and an emphasis on student thinking and problem solving.

The principal in Turin was quick to adopt the New Science and New Math programs. He figured they were neutral enough to keep him out of trouble, nothing like the Rugg curriculum. When the material arrived at the school, there was excitement at first and then bewilderment. Only one of the teachers felt comfortable with math and science and even she had trouble understanding how the new material related to children. The teachers received elegant, beautifully packaged, scientifically sound material that ignored their teaching styles, the organization and structure of their classrooms, and the nature of children. The teachers tried to use what little they understood of the materials, but they complained they didn't have enough time to teach the new program as well as all the other things expected of them.

People in the community reacted to the new material in different ways. Some people, especially those with college degrees or with a desire to have their children become scientists or engineers, were delighted. Others were upset over the de-emphasis of literature, poetry, theater, and the arts. A few kept up the cry of unwarranted government intervention, which had been part of the whole history of public schools in Turin. There was also a concern that drill and memorization was being ignored with all these fancy "modern" ideas. The most common complaint was that the material was so different that you could no longer help your children with their homework.

The sixties and the civil rights movement took most people in Turin by surprise. They had conveniently forgotten that the black members of the community had been struggling to realize their share in the American dream for over 100 years. However, the Burnses were aware of the problems that existed in the school and in the economy. Alice's legacy wouldn't let them forget, and Phillip and his wife, Susan, passed on that sense of decency to their children. In the summer of 1964, during his junior year at the University of Michigan in Ann Arbor, Robert Stokes Burns went to Mississippi with many other whites to support black peoples' struggle for decency and justice. On returning from the Mississippi Freedom Summer, Robert decided that he had to become more involved. One summer wasn't enough. You had to build for the future and the only way to do that was to reach the children. Why not teach and build democracy through the children? Robert chose the way of his grandmother and great grandmother but didn't know it.

When he graduated from Michigan in 1965, Robert decided to get a teaching credential. Things were stirring again. There were Freedom Schools across the South, school boycotts in the cities. The March on Washington called for people to take a pledge, to commit themselves once again to the unfinished task of creating a democratic society. The open classroom was in the air, schools for democracy 1960s' style. Robert took a job teaching in the Hough section of Cleveland. His students were mostly black, all miseducated. After several years he began to discover respectful, creative ways to reach his students, ways confirmed in books like *How Children Learn, The Open Classroom,* and *The Lives of Children.* These books combined with the analysis of the schools presented in *Death at an Early Age, The Way It Spozed to Be, 36 Children* and *How Children Fail,* convinced Robert that he was part of a new movement that could change society through the schools. He was part of a movement but not a new one. Once again the democratic impulse surfaced in public education, cut off from its roots in the common school movement, but with the same values and goals.

Robert met Joanna Berg in Hough. She was teaching third grade and he was the new sixth-grade teacher. They struggled together to undo their students' bitterness about schools, to reach people in the community, and finally, as they felt they were about to succeed, were fired when the parents they worked with lost a major battle with the school district's central administration.

After seven years in Cleveland, Robert asked Joanna if she was willing to go with him to Turin, his hometown, and settle for a while, take some rest and recreation. Robert had been offered a job teaching sixth grade by a friend of his family who was on the school board — and there was also talk of an opening teaching English at the high school that Joanna might be interested in. He admitted to her that the offer was tempting, that he was tired of the struggle, that the songs didn't move him anymore, that there was no fun opposing the war or fighting poverty even though he felt obliged to do it. One night he even confessed that he wanted a child, wanted to be married and to work at being an excellent teacher. So much of their life had been consumed with being in opposition that neither of them felt they had enough time to do what they loved: working with young people. It was difficult for Joanna to admit that she too was fed up with the struggle, but she couldn't keep it from Robert. They knew each other too well to have any but small secrets.

Being tired, wanting to live quietly and do one's work well, seemed like a moral failing, a betrayal of their friends as well as of their deepest beliefs. Yet they were tired, they wanted the adventure of having a child and were afraid that since they were both over thirty it might soon be too late. They decided to try Turin for six months, and stayed.

During the seventies, Robert and Joanna taught quietly and effectively in Turin. Their values didn't change but their style was low-keyed. In 1979, however, it was rumored that Robert was targeted by the Moral Majority as a dangerous influence on children, who had to be removed from his job. A petition was circulated in the community to have him fired for "inappropriate use of materials and inadequate discipline." It also called for a return to "old" teaching methods, drill, strict discipline, and rote learning.

Petitions to the school board are common in Turin. It's part of the Ohio tradition of strong local control of schools. There are usually several petitions circulating the community at any given time. Some deal with removing a textbook that a particular sect or group in the community finds offensive, others have to do with the elimination of electives, the addition of another school bus, the celebration of a new holiday, or the addition of compulsory prayers. They are mostly procedural in content and rarely name individual teachers or administrators. That was the most surprising aspect of the petition against Robert. It not only named him, but was specific about bringing him to a personnel session and having him fired.

Robert and Joanna tried not to worry about the petition until they had more information, but it kept coming up. Robert hadn't done anything differently this year, none of his students' parents was complaining, what wasn't he seeing? Sure, every once in a while he raised criticisms of some of the things going on in the school, but only at formal meetings dealing with educational issues. Maybe some people didn't like his teaching about the civil rights movement or teaching his students about ecology and the need for simple living and self-sufficiency. Maybe they were upset by his giving the students lots of choices and control over their program, but parents didn't have to send their children to his class. In fact, over the last four years a tacit arrangement developed where parents who wanted a very structured program with an emphasis on drill and memorization requested Jim Bagley's class and those who wanted something more open and content-oriented chose his.

Robert's parents knew all about the petition. It was circulated by some of their friends and, as his father tried to explain, wasn't meant as a personal attack on Robert. His class and his way of teaching were symbolic of changes taking place in Turin that were upsetting many of the older people. They didn't understand the ideas of many of the younger parents. In their minds solar energy, the smell of the natural-food store, opposition to nuclear power, and children without discipline were all threats to their way of life. They wanted all classes in the school to be alike and didn't like the way Robert went about teaching, not, his father admitted, that they really knew what Robert was doing or ever bothered to ask him or visit his classroom. The petition was part of a broader effort in the community and the state to ensure conservative domination of public institutions. The petition was aimed at Robert's activities as a citizen, not at his teaching.

"How should I fight back?" That was Robert's sole thought, how to protect what he had carefully built over ten years.

"How should I fight back?"

His father, who was an amazing energetic and coherent eighty-four, answered in a way that surprised him:

"Your grandmother Burns would have known."

Robert never knew his grandmother; she died before he was born.

"What do you mean?"

"We never talked much about Alice. She embarrassed us during her last days. Her mind wasn't here! All of her friends were dead. There's a lot of her in you. Maybe you need to know something about her now."

Robert was getting impatient. He had to develop a strategy, not learn about family history. His father could see his impatience, but nevertheless, persisted and took out a box of letters and clippings.

"Your grandmother, my mother, was a teacher and a troublemaker. Some of these things of hers might be of use to you."

That was how Robert and Joanna got Alice's letters and began to learn about her and Colonel Parker and John Dewey, about her mother Elizabeth, and about the fact that they were part of a nurturing tradition as old as our nation.

Robert's petition never came to a hearing. He had more friends and his ideas had more advocates than he imagined. What emerged from the petition were a series of community forums concentrating on what the common schools in Turin should be in the future.

Once again in Turin as in many other places, urban, rural, and suburban, the schools are the center of community conflict. We have to decide once again what we believe should be basic in public education, remembering that what we consider basic in education cannot be separated from what kind of society we dream of living in. It is not simply a question of whether the schools should return to drill and rote learning or become open. Certainly the basics are at issue, but what has to be understood is that *different parts of the community have different notions of what is basic for children*. All the strands of conflict that existed over the almost 200 years of public education in the United States are still present in Turin and in just about every community in the United States. The struggle to find out what is basic in education is part of the struggle to find out what should be basic to life in the United States. Democracy is our problem, has always been our problem. *There is no "back" in the fantasy of going back to the basics.*

During the late eighteenth century, people were not burdened with the idea that the United States became a democracy as soon as the British surrendered. The problem they faced was how and what kind of a democracy to create. Visions of the future ranged from Hamilton's notion of electing a President for life and having an enlightened monarchy, to Thomas Paine's advocacy of a humanitarian federal democracy controlled by workers. Central to all these visions was the idea of a democratic citizen: a person with the skills, intelligence, and sensitivity to be self-governing and to be a partner in the process of community governance. Debates over education centered on the qualifications for, and quality of citizenship in, the new republic.

To understand the struggles advocates of universal free public education faced and still face, it is crucial to remember that the United States Constitution did not grant full citizenship to slaves, women, or the poor. To be an advocate of education for all people was also to be an advocate of full citizenship for all. It is not surprising that an unusually high proportion of advocates of the common schools were abolitionists, feminists, Socialists and other social progressives. Nor is it surprising that opinions on what should be basic in public education were directly related to people's ideas of citizenship and democracy. The word "basic" was used in its original Greek sense of being a stepping stone, a pedestal, a base, something that led somewhere, that supported or provided a foundation for something else. A basic skill was one that provided a road to a goal, a strength that enabled a certain quality of life to be supported. Basic skills had no meaning without a vision of the goal, not of education per se, but of society. In rethinking what basic skills should be provided for our children, we have to rethink the goals of public education. This means dealing with the same basic question the founders of our republic struggled with: What kind of a democracy are we to become?

I believe that debates about basic skills are not over the nature or quality of education. They are disagreements over what kind of adults we want our children to become and about how much responsibility we are willing to assume for the education of other people's children. The question then is whether we have the will to make democracy happen. Public education has always been a part of our nation's commitment to democracy. The common school of Horace Mann, the school for all the children of all the people, is still worth fighting for if we hope to see our children or grandchildren live in a just, compassionate, and democratic society. There never was a time when public education worked for all the children, but fortunately, there also never was a time in our history when some people weren't struggling to make it work. It is that task that we must continue. It is possible now to build a program for public education, one that combines the best practices of the past with programs that relate to the specific social and technological conditions of our current life. In doing it we must keep in mind that the goal of public education is to provide young people with the basic skills needed to become effective and decent citizens in a democratic society.

·PART THREE·

The Three Rs:
On the Relation Between
Skills and Content

No MATTER HOW THE ISSUE of what should be basic in public education is approached, one has to encounter THE BASIC SKILLS. It is all right to talk about democracy, opportunity, creativity, and other general ideas, but most people insist that, as important as these are, they don't represent *the basics* needed for survival in our society. These basics are, simply put, the ability to read, to calculate, and to write legibly and grammatically. The three Rs, reading, 'riting, and 'rithmetic, are *the* basic skills in most people's minds, and that sentiment has considerable justification. If someone graduates from high school unable to read, write, or calculate, he or she will be at a distinct disadvantage getting a job, voting, knowing about what's happening in the world, and even just getting around.

It's important, however, to consider what kinds of skills reading, writing, and calculating are. Can they be compared to knowing how to use a tape recorder, turn on and tune a television, change a flat tire, or play an electronic computer game? Or are they closer to knowing how to put together a show to tape, select a decent television program to watch, rebuild a car engine, or program a computer? Can the three Rs be mastered mechanically through drill or is there something about reading, writing, and calculating that goes beyond drill and memorization?

Consider reading and writing to start. You read something, and write about something. Reading and writing cannot be separated from meaning of some sort. It is impossible to divorce these skills from the social context in which they are acquired, the content with which they deal, and the uses they are expected to serve in a student's life. *Context, content,* and *use* determine the way the skill is taught and imply the goals that justify acquisition of the skill.

Context

The context in which reading and writing are taught consists of the social setting for learning, the attitudes of teachers and learners, and the structure of the learning program that students encounter. Some different contexts in which reading and writing are taught are:

- a private school in which pupils are expected to read as a matter of course. The teachers are also expected to have all their pupils reading or they will be be questioned and possibly fired by the parent board of directors. The pupils are required to behave properly and attend to their studies or they will be expelled from school.
- a public school in a poor community where teachers are demoralized and expect the majority of their students to fail, and where bits and pieces of many commercial reading programs are used to keep the students busy.
- a home where parents choose to teach their own children. The materials are the books from the parents' library, and the teaching takes place after dinner around the kitchen table.
- a Hebrew school where some reading has to be mastered in order for the child to be initiated into the world of adults.
- a newly created nation where literacy is considered essential to development and survival, and is taught to young people at their workplaces.

Content

The content of reading and writing has to do with what is in the books children read and with the kind of written statements students are expected to make. Content can vary, so that in the third grade, eight-year-olds may encounter classical mythology, insulting and racist texts, Tolstoy, the Old Testament, or technical manuals.

Use

The use of reading and writing also varies according to the educational expectations of adults. For some youngsters, passing reading simply makes them immune to the humiliation of being left back and put in with younger children. For others it is a source of knowledge and personal pleasure, while for those in developing countries it can be a path out of poverty for their families and themselves.

Context, content, and use define specific conceptions of what reading and writing are. These skills cannot be separated out and looked at as "pure." Trying to reduce reading to knowing the sounds of letters is like confusing the ability to play scales with the ability to play a song; trying to reduce writing to handwriting and the knowledge of a few grammatical conventions is like confusing copying sheet music with composing a song.

The context, content, and use of reading, for example, are determined by the goals that are set for the learner. Here are a few examples of how reading and writing are inextricably connected with social, political, and moral goals.

I. Schools for Competition

Goal
To help children become competitive in a harsh world with limited resources and understand that not everyone will be able to make it.

Implications for Defining What the Skill of Reading Is and How It Is to Be Taught

CONTEXT: A program with these goals must have a grading system that measures students against each other. Reading must become a quantifiable skill. Success in competition must be rewarded, failure considered a sign of inferiority. Some failure and some success is necessary in order to maintain the structure. There should be an emphasis on the way things must be done. Following the correct procedure should be almost as important as getting the correct answer. The questioning of authority, whether teacher or text, should be discouraged and even punished.

CONTENT: The content must appear to be factual. Questions should have single answers and be generated by text or teacher. Things that involve questioning or that lead to genuine differences of opinion should be avoided. Texts that confirm current school and business authority should be encouraged. The content should support the values of competition as well as current social structure.

USE: Reading should be used to accept facts as presented in print, to learn to follow written directions, to learn skills from manuals, to get current information from newspapers and magazines, and to help students "get ahead."

This might seem like an extreme and unduly severe sketch of reading, yet the idea that schools must teach students to adjust to "the real world" is quite common. It embodies the idea that our society will have its rich and its poor and that students must learn to find their proper place in a world that neither will, nor should, change.

Here's a portrait of a "reality-oriented" classroom that a friend's child has been forced to attend. John is a fifth grader. His teacher believes that school should teach children to adjust to the harsh realities of competition. In order to do this she instituted a token money system into class. At the beginning of the school year she gives every child $100 in play money. She tells the students that during the school year they can earn more money or lose what they have, just as adults do in the real world. Money is to be earned according to the student's performance on tests and assignments. An A is worth $10, a B, $7, a C, $5, and a D, $1. Failing grades earn nothing. In return, there are aspects of life in the classroom that have to be paid for. If you have to sharpen your pencil during a lesson it costs $5, and if you have to go to the toilet during a lesson it costs $4. Also if you do something wrong you can pay anywhere from $5 to $50 to avoid your punishment. Whenever you accumulate $1,500, you win a free ice cream cone and start again at $100.

My friend's son, John, is a good student. He likes to learn, has good bowel habits, and writes with a light hand so he never breaks his pencil. To his dismay, during the first few months of school, he accumulated money and resentment from his classmates at an unprecedented rate. He didn't strive for the money rewards, had spent most of his life in school situations where the reward of learning was knowing something new. The money became a problem. His friends wanted to borrow some. Some students said they needed it to sharpen their pencils; others wanted it to get ahead. The worst students in the class, the ones most likely to break their pencils or need to pee because of the anxiety they experienced in performing, turned out naturally to be the poorest ones in the class. Ironically, most of the students who were poor in class money came from some of the poorest families in the community. For them school was a verification of poverty rather than a route out of it.

At times some of the poor students wanted to borrow money from John, but it was clear to him and to them that they would never earn enough to pay him back. This led to his giving some money away and having some stolen. Some of the poorest students would rather take the risk of stealing than spend a school year in debt. And John faced a final dilemma when he achieved the magical $1,500. All he would get was a thirty-five cent ice cream cone and he would have to start all over again in the system with $100. It was better to hover somewhere around $1,100, pretend he was poor, and function with an awareness that he was rich, than blow it all and start again. He was in the real world, or at least that's what his teacher said. One particularly bad day he earned enough money to go over $1,500, had $600 stolen, broke a pencil on purpose, couldn't stand his classmates' snide remarks about his being a smartass, and really wanted to read an interesting book, without worrying about how much play money he'd receive for reading it. He told his mother that he couldn't read or do any work in class anymore. All he thought about was that damn money system.

Finally, in a fit of frustration, he took all of his accumulated wealth out of his desk and raised his hand. When the teacher finally recognized him he tore the money up and threw it in the air. The next day his mother was called to school. She was asked to meet with the teacher and the school psychologist. Obviously there had to be something wrong with John for him to act so defiantly.

At the meeting the teacher was very pleasant and sympathetic. She asked if John was under stress at home, if there was something she or the psychologist could help with. John's mother replied that John's problem was in school, that he couldn't stand the social pressure that the money system created. Moreover, she argued, it was the school's role to teach reading, not to control her child and force him into a competitive system against his will. The psychologist intervened at that point and replied, "Mrs. Taylor, along with all the other responsibilities we have, it is our job to teach children to adjust to our society. The money system is an accurate reflection of our society."

At that point John's mother, Eve, who is an active feminist, exploded. "Listen, this society is sexist. Does that mean that your job is to teach the boys to be sexist and the girls to accept an inferior role? There is racism in the society. Does that mean you teach whites to be racist and blacks to believe they are inferior? There are poor people. Does that mean that you teach some children that they deserve to be poor and others that they deserve wealth?"

The psychologist tried to calm Eve down and the principal was called in. Eve's impression was that the only concern the two of them had was to protect the teacher. She told me that she walked out somewhere in the middle of a sentence that went something like "Our teachers are professionals and we need your support in helping children learn how to take a positive role in our programs."

Eve pulled John out of school and sent him to live with his father in Arizona where the public schools seemed to be less crazy. She is bitter about John's terrible times in school, and the powerlessness she felt in trying to make the officials understand what her son had to live through.

What she experienced, however, is not uncommon. Reading, writing, and other school-related skills are, and must be, tied into a social and moral system in the classroom. If you don't approve of the system or if your child can't fit into the system comfortably, you'll be trapped. If you try to explain this to teachers or administrators, they'll deny that moral or social issues are at stake. Instead of open democratic dialogue leading to a mutual resolution of problems, irreconcilable differences develop that lead to people pulling their children out of school.

II. Schools to Make Good Christians

Goals

Eve's complaint was, among other things, that the school was not democratic enough. Other people pull their children out of school for the opposite reason, that the public schools are too democratic. Many of the Christian schools that have opened recently are explicit about their desire to teach Christianity as established truth. The goals of these schools are to make their students good Christians, to have them respect adult authority and the received Word and be able to quote Scripture as an aid to action, and finally to protect students from evolutionism, atheism, scientism, and communism. These goals have clear implications for defining what the skills of reading and writing are and how they are to be taught. Despite the claims of many of these schools to be basic three-Rs schools, their curriculum is content-laden and their structure pervaded by authoritarian values.

Implications

CONTEXT: According to this view, the Bible is the source of truth, and reading it is more important than reading anything else. The context is one of the battles to defend fundamentalist truth in a world of too many nonbelievers. The child is to be propagandized, though this is not thought of as propaganda. It is more that the child is to be initiated into the truth and must be punished if he or she will not receive it. The context is at one time both loving and hostile. The message of love *must* be conveyed and, within the system, reading means different things according to the text. One must read the Bible with acceptance, but must read Darwin with bitterness or, better yet, avoid Darwin altogether. Reading is not to give open-ended access to the world. It is a tool for the confirmation of belief.

CONTENT: The content is Christian — all subjects must reflect what are called Christian truths. Other content must be criticized in the light of the Bible and fundamentalist texts. There is some content that is simply prohibited. Reading had best be confined to Christian texts, or mechanical exercises devoid of social or scientific content that might question fundamentalist Christian beliefs. In extreme cases, this leads to the following rather frightening attack on content:

BOOK-BURNING CEREMONY BY CHURCH SCHOOL
Students at a private Omaha school watched yesterday as their principal set fire to a pile of books that included an issue of *National Geographic* and Daffy Duck comics.

They are distractions that could "hinder Christian lives," said the Rev. Lars Wessberg, principal of Omaha Christian School.

Publications thrown into the flames included Batman and Daffy Duck comic books, the *National Geographic,* a record album cover showing the rock group Animals and a book called *50 True Tales of Terror.*

Wessberg said he considered his action "symbolic," and said children attending his private school brought the material to be burned.

The principal quoted from the Bible as the books burned, reading from the Book of Acts: "And not a few of them that practiced magical arts brought their books together and burned them in the sight of all . . ."

"I believe as a Christian school we have a responsibility to uphold Christian values in every area of life," he said.

One student, 15-year-old Randy Ham, said he brought nothing to burn because he owned no material he considered distracting.

"But I think this is a good idea," the boy said. "You can't live for God if you are not dedicated."[30]

A lot of fundamentalist pressure on public schools is made in the guise of a call for a return to the basics. Actually the call for drill, rote learning, and memorization is an attack on current content. The issue is not whether students are doing worse in reading now than in the past so much as that they are reading texts that contain ideas that a moralistic minority considers dangerous.

USE: One reads to confirm one's views of the world. It can be a powerful weapon in the defense of faith, but it can also lead one astray. The importance of reading should not be exaggerated.

III. Schools for Thinking

Goals
A third view of reading, one that I hold and that has been identified with progressive and open education, considers

reading to be a source of personal pleasure and power, as well as a way for groups of people to share ideas and aspirations. According to this view, students should be able to read anything they choose, should be encouraged to think critically about the content of what they read, come to enjoy reading as a source of pleasure, and learn how to use books to enrich personal and group life.

It is important to emphasize that this view is an assertion of the basic importance of reading, and not one that says students don't have to learn to read if they don't want to. This last simplification of open education is frequently used in debates over the basics and too often accepted uncritically. It is possible to believe in the free choice of reading material, and to emphasize thought and pleasure, and still believe reading is basic.

Implications

CONTEXT: The context of reading consistent with these goals would be cooperative rather than competitive. Children would not be ranked and would be encouraged to assist one another. A single developmental program would be discouraged, though the teaching of individual skills when needed would occur. There would be opportunity for open-ended discussion and every lesson would not have to be tied up with a definite conclusion. Intelligent disagreement would be encouraged and emphasis would be put on active participation of students in planning their reading programs and learning to make choices. Adult authority would be respected, but questioning would be encouraged and differences of opinion not settled by the quick and forceful application of adult authority.

CONTENT: Diverse content would be encouraged. Books dealing with complex social, political, and personal issues would be read and debated. Scientific controversies, questions of the relations of science and religion, of loyalty to family and to the state, of the development of ideas and opinions would be read about and discussed. A wide variety of reading material would make up the core of the curriculum, and content rather than mechanical exercises would be emphasized.

USE: Reading would be for personal pleasure and empowerment. It would be done critically so that the reader would know how to judge what is read. Poor reading skills would consist of being able to sound out words and not understand what you read, and believing everything you read, or believing something because some authority or book insists you believe it.

These three portraits are somewhat caricatured. Few programs draw the lines as finely as I did. Yet they illustrate an essential aspect of the debate over what should be basic in education. The issue is not reading, writing, or arithmetic, as is often stated. It is the quality of life and the nature of society. No core that could be called the essence of reading can be isolated and considered common to the three positions described. There have been attempts to do this but I believe they are theoretically and not merely practically doomed to failure. For example, one popular academic view of reading, which on the surface seems plausible, asserts that reading is simply decoding. The object of basic reading programs should be to teach the skill of decoding, that is, going from written letters to words and sounds, no more or less.

First consider the meaning of decoding in the context of reading English. To decode you have to have a code, some dictionary of symbols that when put together and understood through some key (or series of rules of interpretation) produce the equivalents of words or sentences. The alphabet in English is the basic symbol vocabulary, and the rules of sound-letter equivalents and of semantics provide the key to decoding. In simple terms, reading consists of going from something written down on a page to something with meaning that can also be spoken. At this point we begin to run into trouble. What is written down to decode? Who decides upon the text? What dialect is chosen as the proper decoding? Are words merely to be decoded or are sentences and paragraphs to be decoded too? Are the meanings of the words expected to be mastered? Is one reading if one pronounces sentences correctly but doesn't understand them? What are the grounds on which one decides that a person reads adequately or not: do we have at this point to introduce a view of the content, context, and use of reading in order to talk about what reading is?

I believe we do. We cannot go far even in something so apparently innocent as decoding before we get to context, meaning, content, interpretation, and thought. And these lead beyond reading itself to larger conceptions of education and its role in personal life and in society. There is no abstraction called "reading" that can be isolated and taught no matter what we believe. People, and that naturally includes children, are context, content, use, and goal bound. You cannot pull basic skills out of life and reach "pure" education. At bottom, the teaching of reading and other skills involves moral as well as technical issues. It is a question of what young people should know, what resources and ideas they should be exposed to, and what opportunities they are given to become active and welcome members of the adult world.

Myths of Learning

By ignoring context, content, and use, and therefore avoiding issues of belief and politics, a number of myths have developed about how learning problems should be solved. These myths represent attempts to solve problems relating to the quality and meaning of life through the manipulation of people or their environment. Here are some common myths:

1. *More time spent on reading, writing, and arithmetic means learning more reading, writing, and arithmetic.* Consider this hypothetical statement made by a principal to parents worried about low reading scores in their school: "I am glad we have had this dialogue about our school's reading problems. There is no question that we can do better, and the staff agrees that we'll have to put in an extra effort to reach all of the children. From now on every child will get an extra half hour of reading and an extra half hour of math. We will set up intensive reading labs for students who still have problems. We need your help so our work can be reinforced at home."

This structural myth embodies the larger social myth that bigger is better. There is no reason to assume that larger doses of unsuccessful teaching will cure anything. There are also saturation points that have to be respected in learning situations. If one is required to do something for too long a time, fatigue, boredom, and resentment can interfere with learning. There are probably situations where more time spent on basics means less learning. However, to assert that more is not necessarily better is not to deny the importance of reading, writing, and math. It is simply a warning against pseudosolutions to serious problems. Put quite simply, if you can't stand reading, and being in your classroom gives you a stomach- or headache, being forced to remain in the room and read for a longer time won't solve your problem.

2. *Smaller class size means better learning;* and *The more teacher aides we have the better the learning.* Millions of dollars have been wasted in support of these two related myths, strongly advocated by teachers and their organizations. Many teachers' organizations make smaller class size their main nonmonetary demand. In the sixties, the New York City schools experimented with the MES (More Effective School) program, the central component of which

was to reduce class size. Those of us who worked at or had the opportunity to observe schools using the program, referred to them as MESS schools. There was no reason to believe that ineffectual teachers would be any better with a smaller number of students. In fact an ineffectual teacher can have a worse influence on members of a small class than on a big class. The old saw "there's safety in numbers" can be very meaningful for a child trying to hide from a bad teacher.

The reason reducing class size (or equivalently, bringing in aides to relieve the burden on the teacher) has become so popular in teaching circles is that it avoids all questions of responsibility and the quality of teaching. All members of a teachers' organization can agree upon it. It does not create friction within the organization and allows every teacher to continue on a smaller scale what he or she had been doing on a larger scale.

The quest for smaller classes goes back to the late nineteenth century, when classes of over a hundred students were not uncommon and fifty students was considered a light load. In that time, smaller class size was intricately bound up with other educational reform: with the development of experience-oriented curriculum, with the development of settlement houses and other social services, and with the broadening of the curriculum to include the arts and community life. Angelo Patri, for example, in his book *A Schoolmaster of the Great City,* describes how the struggle in 1906 to reduce classes to a manageable size only made sense in the context of changing teachers' attitudes and community involvement. Certainly there are sensible constraints on class size, though it is not clear what they are. Nor is it clear that having all classes in all subjects and in all grades the same size is the most efficient or economical way of organizing learning. However, when the reduction of class size is elevated to the position of *the* solution to educational problems, we are in the realm of myth.

The same problem exists when aides are depended on to solve educational problems. Most often teacher aides are used to grade papers, do paperwork, or sit with students who are difficult to manage in class. They are used to make teachers' lives easier, not to improve the quality of instruction and learning.

3. *Motivation.* There is another group of myths dealing with how children learn that center around the question of motivation. They could be called the Calvin-Rousseau-Skinner myths and deal with individual learners divorced from the content, context, and use of what is learned. There are three main variants of this myth deriving from Calvin, Rousseau, and B. F. Skinner.

CALVIN: The Calvinist version presumes that children are basically lazy and mischievous. They have to be kept in line, and motivated by the threat of punishment. Strict discipline in this view motivates learning. An extreme version of this position states that strict discipline not merely motivates learning but actually *produces* it.

ROUSSEAU: The Rousseauian view is softer and is embodied in this quote from Rousseau's *Émile:* "The greatest, most important, most useful rule of education is DO NOT SAVE TIME, BUT LOSE IT." For Rousseau, losing time is equivalent to preserving the purity of the child and letting him or her grow according to natural internal laws of development. Motivation to grow and learn comes from within and should not be interfered with by adult demands. The adult should present a supporting, rich environment and step out of the way. In an extreme version, the Rousseauian view claims that culture corrupts, and strict discipline, instead of producing motivation, destroys it.

SKINNER: Under the Skinnerian view the child is neither depraved nor saintly, but neutral, a creature in need of rewards in order to function. Rewards mediate learning in that one learns in order to get a reward that satisfies a basic biological or social need. Candy can get you to read. The motivation is provided by the candy, the learning is an intermediate step, a consequence of the drive to get the reward.

It is interesting to note that these three views of motivation have deep roots in traditions of Western thinking. One is theological, another humanistic, and the third, scientific. The battle between theology, secular humanism, and scientism often plays itself out in education over disagreements on how to motivate children and view the adult role in the process of motivation.

All three views tend to confuse learning with the notion of being motivated to learn. It is quite possible, however, to be motivated to learn something (for whatever reason) and still not learn it. A person might want to learn how to play an instrument and have no access to the instrument, or to do math and have a confusing text and unclear teacher and not learn. In considering the myths of motivation it is important to keep in mind that *being motivated to learn and actually learning are different things;* that when someone says that *the* most important part of learning is motivation, they have stated at best a partial truth.

All three motivation myths state these partial truths:

If you are not motivated you won't learn
AND
If you are motivated you will learn.

Both of these assertions assume that motivation is a general phenomenon. This assumption is quite common in discussions about learning. A student "is motivated" or "isn't motivated," must "be motivated," "needs motivation." A teacher must "create motivation," "provide motivation," "instill motivation." However, the issue is more complicated. A student may not be motivated to read in a particular classroom with a particular teacher but may be motivated to read in another context. Similarly someone may not be motivated to behave in a polite and sensitive way in a social situation that is considered oppressive, but may behave perfectly well elsewhere. Whenever someone says, "X is not motivated," it is important to pursue the issue and ask, "Not motivated to do what, when, where, how, and with what other people?"

There is some sense in all three views, however, and we need to balance them against each other rather than become bogged down in nonresolvable argumentation. There are times when discipline invites defiance just as there are times when freedom leds to disorder and rewarding behavior leads to bribery. Coercion, neglect, and indulgence, other words for the extremes of discipline, freedom, and reinforcement, can generate learning problems as easily as solve them. For example, neither freedom nor discipline nor reward will motivate a defiant bored child to learn anything.

It makes sense to maximize the joy without forgetting that some learning is boring, some frustrating, and some outright painful. It also makes sense to remember that some complex and sophisticated things can be mastered joyfully.

Many times debates over "the basics" turn into arguments among the pain, pleasure, and reward people. However, all sides are right, in a way. Significant learning involves hard work and discipline. It also involves play, experimentation, discovery, reward, and fun. For the sake of health and sanity it pays to maximize the pleasure. It also pays to look beyond motivation to the content, the quality of instruction, the social context of learning, and the use of what is learned in the student's life to understand when student motivation leads to learning rather than frustration.

The mechanical and motivational changes represented by the educational myths have not succeeded in revitalizing public education. Yet they are still the main answers one hears in debates about basic skills and the current state of public education. The answer is discipline, the answer is motivation, the answer is freedom, the answer is smaller classes, the answer is back to the basics. But what are the goals of public education and what finally is basic? Shouldn't we try to start once again, respectful of the past, and try to define what the function of public education is in a society that is trying to achieve democracy? What are the basic skills our children need, now, at the end of the twentieth century, to help them become decent people and citizens, and happy adults? We have to answer these questions. *There is no point in bothering with public education if you don't believe in democracy.* If you do, then Thomas Jefferson's commitment to public education must be yours, too:

> I look to the diffusion of light and education as the re-
> sources most to be relied on for ameliorating the condition,
> promoting the virtue, and advancing the happiness of man.
> And I do hope, in the present spirit of extending to the great
> mass of mankind the blessings of instruction, I see a prospect
> of great advancement in the happiness of the human race,
> and this may proceed to an indefinite, although not an infi-
> nite, degree. A system of general instruction, which shall
> reach every description of our citizens, from the richest to
> the poorest, as it was the earliest, so shall it be the latest of
> all the public concerns in which I shall permit myself to take
> an interest.[31]

PART FOUR

The Basics

W<small>HAT ARE THE BASIC SKILLS</small> involved in democratic citizenship? What should we offer our children and what should we expect of them? We have to decide what these skills are, and we must also create a program for our schools where these skills are taught within a democratic context, with diverse content, and a sensitivity to the use of the skills offered. We must also decide upon priorities and possibilities: what skills are most important and what can we do now when a high regard for democracy is all too uncommon? I believe it is possible to continue in the tradition of all those women and men who have tried to empower all the children of all our people through public education. In that spirit, and borrowing from past practice, I will attempt to articulate what basic skills we should offer our children and suggest ways to go about remaking our public schools. It is a way of opening up, once again, central questions that have faced this nation throughout our history: how can we become a democracy? What can we do to create an educated, decent citizenry? What can we offer our children so they can grow strong and join us in our commitment to build a democracy? And finally, what can we do to overcome the helplessness so many of us feel to influence the events that shape our lives and the lives of our children?

The basic skills are those skills needed to be an effective citizen in our democracy now, at the end of the twentieth century. They arise from the technological and social conditions of our time but are based on the fundamental moral ideas of democracy. For me the principles that are fundamental in a democracy are:

1. *Everyone should have access to information and re-*

sources and be informed about how to use them. Without knowing what is happening in the world or without techniques to organize the flood of information available to us, we become powerless to act intelligently. And without resources we can't act. Young people need to learn how to gather and organize information, as well as understand what resources are available and how they can acquire and use them. This ranges from learning to read intelligently, write coherently, and calculate efficiently, to simple things like finding out how much money you earn for different jobs and what skills you need to get the jobs, to more complex things like finding someone to teach you a skill you want to acquire when your family and friends don't have any way to help you.

2. *People should have as much control over their own lives as is consistent with not damaging others.* This implies that maximum individual freedom must be allowed for, consistent with social coherence. Decisions affecting people's lives should be made from the bottom up — those people affected by a decision should have a voice in that decision whenever possible. Hierarchies should be avoided unless absolutely necessary. Mutual respect is essential to democracy and cannot develop where hierarchies dominate.

This implies that young people should know something about control, should have opportunity to exercise power, and analyze the consequences of it. They should understand what it means to damage others and should study the line between individual freedom and harming others. They also should understand that differences of culture, style, and taste should not be viewed as threatening. They should have practice making decisions affecting their lives both personally and as a group and be able to analyze social situations so that sensible decisions can be made or foolish ones revised. Finally, they should be able to analyze social structures, understand what hierarchies are, and consider whether they are necessary. They should also understand their own strengths and the strengths of their fellows. Mutual respect should be a major goal of education. From such respect effective personal and social action should emerge.

3. *Everyone should consider carefully the balance between fulfillment in their personal lives and service to others.* It is fundamental in a democracy that service be not merely an obligation but a source of personal and social renewal. This implies that young people should experience cooperative work, should have an opportunity to learn in the community as well as in the classroom, and should come to understand how learning itself can be a lifelong source of growth and pleasure.

These three principles of democratic living suggest three basic goals for public education. These goals are to help young people

- learn to acquire, organize, and analyze information
- learn how to get access to resources and have command over them
- learn how to act effectively personally and with others
- learn how to renew oneself, be a source of renewal to others, and contribute to sustaining and renewing the earth as well.

Each of these basic goals can be translated into educational programs. I believe that creating such programs could counter the current demoralization within our public schools and give students, teachers, and parents the spirit, focus, energy, and power needed to reconstruct public education. This would imply opening oneself up to new definitions of basic skills and, rather than dreaming of returning to a utopian past that never existed, accepting the present challenge of building a powerful system of public education as part of a reaffirmation of faith in our ability to create a democracy.

The skills required to deal with information, act effectively, and balance self-fulfillment with service to others are what could be called whole-life skills. They require development of all the faculties: of imagination, language, and feeling as well as the intellect. They also demand active participation in learning and experimentation, as well as in the more usual school-related skills such as memorization. It is possible to design eductional programs that incorporate all of these skills, and I would like to propose one such program that focuses on six basic skills. I hope that other people will also take up the same challenge of revitalizing the commitment of public education to the development of democracy in the United States and that many programs will be designed and many people will dare to try them out.

Six Basic Skills

There are at least six basic skills that our children must acquire if they are to learn how to function effectively and compassionately as adults. They are:

1. The ability to use language well and thoughtfully. This skill implies developing speech that is sensitive to the weight and meaning of words, acquiring the habit of reading intelligently and critically, and learning to write coherently in forms that can be read by others. The struggle to say what one means and the ability to attend to the meaning of other people's words must be central to any educational program that hopes to develop democratic sensibility.

2. The ability to think through a problem and experiment with solutions. This skill implies learning techniques of observation, questioning, listening, and experimenting. It also implies that modes of thinking should be taught explicitly and not merely implied through different school subjects.

3. The ability to understand scientific and technological ideas and to use tools. This implies learning to use numbers, computers, and hammers, and having opportunities to apply language and thinking skills to scientific, technical, and mechanical problems.

4. *The ability to use the imagination* and participate in and appreciate different forms of personal and group expression. This implies serious attention be given to the arts from historical, performance, and technical perspectives.

5. *The ability to understand how people function in groups* and to apply that knowledge to group problems in one's own life.

6. *The ability to know how to learn something yourself* and to have the skills and confidence to be a learner all your life. This involves learning how to deal with new situations, and to develop new skills and interests throughout your life.

These six basic skills lead to a six-stranded curriculum that suggests ways of reorganizing the structure of public education and making fundamental changes in the way students are treated. I will discuss each of the six basic skills separately and then suggest concrete ways in which, even in these difficult times, positive changes might be made in public education.

BASIC SKILL 1:
The Ability to Use Language Well and Thoughtfully

Reading without critical understanding and writing without the ability to express what you intend are not basic skills: reading thoughtfully and writing with control of content are basic skills. Underlying these basic skills is the ability to use language well.

It is crucial to understand the intimate relationship between content and comprehension. Young people have to learn to attend to the meaning of what they read, to compare it with other material, to question the author, to guess at intent, or challenge conclusions. They need to deal with the substance of, rather than simply pronounce the sounds of, letters on the page. Reading is understanding, not reciting.

The same is true for writing. The mechanical skills are only useful if they serve meaning and content. *Reading and writing as basic skills cannot be separated from understanding.* This implies that *understanding is itself a basic skill* and that it is essential that time be devoted to conversation, observation, analysis, experimentation, and other activities that lead to comprehension. These are not frills, or wastes of time, as some people assert, but are at the very core of developing intelligent reading, coherent writing and informed citizenship.

Language is a form of mobility. Through listening and reading one can explore spatial, temporal, and imaginative worlds that are beyond what one can observe directly. A major reason to learn to listen and to read is to become aware of the world outside of one's own experience. In cultures that do not use written language, speech is the central means of preserving history and sharing adult knowledge of the world with the young. If a child doesn't learn how to listen, to attend to nuances of meaning, there is the chance that he or she might make a major social error or lack a skill necessary to adult survival. In our society, writing supplements speaking as a source of information and experience. Through books and magazines, et cetera, it is possible to project oneself through space and time, and share the imaginative work (artistic, scientific, and technical) of people one will never hear or meet.

Speaking and listening, and writing and reading, are obviously powerful ways of acquiring information about the world. Yet most school programs discourage speech, pay no attention to the development of sophisticated listening skills, turn writing into mechanical exercises, and impoverish the content of reading. The opposite should happen. Speech, especially student speech, should be encouraged. That's not the same as encouraging talking out in the middle of a lesson or shouting wildly and incoherently, as some fundamentalists would interpret it. Rather it means that students should be encouraged to speak in class about their perceptions of the world, about their ideas and aspirations, about adult politics and religion, about conflicts they experience and ways they've found of building things and enjoying themselves. Equally, students should be encouraged to listen to each other, raise questions, and speculate in class. *Time must be taken for speech.* This should be a major principle of curriculum development and is essential for the development of intelligent reading and writing programs. *The struggle to say what one means and the ability to attend to the meaning of other people's words are central to an education program that has as a goal the development of democratic sensibility.*

The content of speech and books, the stuff one can talk and read about, should be made clear to young people. Information can be gotten from people if one asks, and from books if one reads, and this bit of information itself should be demonstrated in school by the constant presence of people with things to talk about and by the presence in every class of a rich library that students are encouraged to use.

I did not come from a book-rich home, though there were many adults around who told wonderful tales and were willing to share what they knew with young people. For years in school, books were a problem to me. I had no idea what was in them. Reading was something I was forced to do for some mystical adult reasons having to do with my future. Fortunately, in the fifth or sixth grade I had a teacher who loved books for how they expanded her life, and she shared the knowledge of what was in them with us. This may be my fantasy, but I seem to remember her holding up a book a day and asking our class if we knew what was in it. It was like a wrapped toy, a gift that might contain all kinds of riches. We guessed from the look of the cover and the author's photo on the flap of the jacket. Amazingly, she let us spin out fantasies of what could be in books, let us talk and forget about being self-conscious or nervous about getting the right answer. And then she gave us a peek, read some select paragraph or page, and asked who wanted to read the book first. Usually there was a rush of seven or ten people to grab the book. I remember the crazy feeling of rushing to grab a book. There was something in it, it wasn't the print but the content that made sense of reading to me. In a way, the word *information* is too cold and limited to describe what can be learned from books and from other people. It implies a passive receiving of facts, when reading is really more like the process of in-formation: the structuring, questioning, and evaluating of information that is beyond what you directly experience.

There are a number of ways to structure experience and the accurate thoughtful use of language is a central one. Words are, in the phrase of Arnold Wesker, the British playwright, definitions of experience. When used with attention to meaning, nuance, and context, they are tools that can be used to examine experience and information. When used carelessly or thoughtlessly they can lead to confusion and powerlessness. They can also be deliberately used to deceive as was the case during the Vietnam War when U.S. aggression was described by such phrases as "massive retaliation," "pacification," "incursion," and so on.

Unfortunately, many people are suffering linguistic impoverishment because of the deceitful language of business advertising and politics, and because of the impoverishment of content and the absence of speech in the classroom. Arnold Wesker, in his extraordinary essay *Words as Definitions of Experience,* tells a personal story about the effects of this impoverishment of language:

> One day my eldest son, aged thirteen then, was standing outside his school talking to some friends. It's a local school with a 70% immigrant and working-class population. He's a big boy, who — it was three years ago — had very long hair and those irritatingly happy, intelligent eyes. Two older boys from the school approached him. One kicked him in the back-side. He ignored the kick. "Get stuffed!" said the other

boy to him. "Alright, I will," replied my obliging son, and he continued to ignore the two fourth-formers. "Get stuffed!" said the other boy again. My son assured him, confidently, that as he'd promised, he *would* "get stuffed." The boy drew back his arm and with a heavy ringed fist smashed into my son's right eye. "Good God!" said my son, reeling back, unable to believe anyone could do that or that it could happen to him. And then he came home.

His bewilderment is perhaps what distressed me most. It seemed to him to have no logic, no reason, no point. He couldn't account for it.

He was not equipped with those concepts of human behaviour which might have enabled him to place their actions within a pattern of behaviour recognisable enough for him to have worked out some effective or self-reassuring response. Words contain within them concepts of human behaviour. He was not equipped with such words. . . .

How does my son know whether the punch in the eye was a mere casual act of thuggery, or whether resentments were at work there which neither the bullies nor my son understood? How do youngsters measure their experience? What (and this is fundamental) has education formulated to enable such measurements to be made?[32]

Wesker's son is not the only young person at a loss for words. I have worked with too many young people who simply cannot express what they want, think, or feel. They are unaccustomed to using language as a vehicle for the expression of thought. They have little opportunity to discuss the world or themselves. School negates the expression of thought or feeling and in some ways impoverishes it. Students learn spelling but never spend time weighing the meaning and use of words. They memorize word definitions and are tested on their "new vocabulary" without ever having considered the context in which their vocabulary words have power or the reasons some people had to invent those words. Again we are faced with the impoverishment of content, this time on the level of words. There has to be a way to make concern for language a priority in the schools. *The ability to use language well and thoughtfully is a basic skill.* I propose that time and energy be spent on developing a curriculum that deals with words as vehicles for understanding and communicating experience accurately and sensitively. The subject which should be taught at all grade levels could be called *Word Definitions of Experience,* after a suggestion Wesker makes in his pamphlet, which is similar to what I propose. Wesker says that his concern

> is to defend language as a means of both naming and comprehending the implications of the experience of *what is being done to one, and what one is doing to others.* And I believe it is the teacher who must help identify and define experience by using language in a special subject set aside in the school curriculum, and that he must do so with the aid of the works of artists.[33]

He then gives examples of what might be taught in such a subject:

> Let me illustrate this. Take a word like "intimidate." Intimidation describes a sensation some people feel, and a behaviour others enact. And the fear, unease, confusion *felt* by the one, and the menace, distress, insecurity *caused* by the other, must surely be among the most basic of experiences which people meet in their everyday relationships one to another. Now, is there a moment in any school where an imaginative, fully trained teacher takes that word in front of a class and shakes it inside out for its meaning, for its appearance in the contemporary world, in history, or — most important — for application to the pupil's own life? I'm not talking about a half an hour devoted to discussing the meaning of the word. Nor of a lesson. But of perhaps a whole month, two lessons a week. Eight sessions devoted to one word, and using for illustration the rich fields of painting, literature, and film. At the end of the first year: eight words. At the end of six years: nearly fifty words.

Words! Vindictive. Lilliputian. Mockery. Superficial. Spurious. Greed. Relativity. Tolerance. Doubt. Reason. Faith. Freedom. Demagogue. . . . A linguistic survival kit!

It's not simply a question of building up a vocabulary about which the child may boast but of fitting together the jigsaw of experience, of building a battery of concepts. I don't know what those words should be. Individuals with other qualifications could list such an initial vocabulary for understanding the human condition. I do not say guaranteeing an understanding of the human condition. Nothing can guarantee that! But a basis, upon which there exists a possibility for understanding. That basis, that "beginner's kit" must be possible to evolve. Men and women have built essential words over centuries, giving names to their actions and sensations, pinning them down for all time. And when once a word was found inadequate, another was found to describe the nuance.

There's the challenge! How many words belong to such a basic list? Is it fifty? A hundred? And what would they be? What would be the first dozen words you'd want your child to understand? . . .

And where does one start? What should be the first word? Since we are dealing with words as concepts, then should the word "concept" be the very first word we struggle to make the eleven-year-old child comprehend? Is the eleven-year-old mind able to comprehend such an abstract concept as 'conceptualising'? I'm not qualified to answer that with confidence; but I would have thought that — as an example — the freedom to follow one's own individual conscience is a concept that can be illustrated from much in literature. Some illustrations? Take Ibsen's *An Enemy of the People;* or the film, *On the Waterfront;* or in history, the story of Luther; and in contemporary life, the trade-union closed-shop disputes; and from science, the story of Galileo.[34]

I propose that we take up Wesker's challenge, that art, literature, film, all forms of human expression, be brought together to illuminate experience, and even go further and include learning to read and write as subskills in a content-oriented language program. Such a program would deal with what language can do or express, with the power of saying and writing what you mean and the danger of being fooled by other people's language.

Word Definitions of Experience would begin with intelligent speech and move to reading and writing through an understanding of the power and danger of language. It would give students an opportunity to talk, read, and write about how people live and dream about living, about such things as respect, humor, honesty, rage, excuses, morality, and legality. It would put phonics and grammar in perspective as simple techniques that allow thought to be communicated, and give speech and thinking their proper central role.

The study of *Word Definitions of Experience* could help students understand their place in the world. It could also give them a vocabulary they could use to describe and analyze information in all areas of the curriculum as well as have fun with language.

Word Definitions of Experience could replace what is now called language arts. For young children (five through seven), techniques such as those described in Sylvia Ashton-Warner's *Teacher* could be used. Children could choose their own words, learn, of course, to spell and write them, but most importantly to think about them and use them to tell stories and describe their own experiences.

For older students, *Word Definitions of Experience* could study language as well as literature and deal with such topics as

- the history of uniform spelling and the evolution of language
- rules of language and their variations
- linguistic conventions and writers who break the rules
- the working habits of writers.

In the context of this class, grammar and spelling could be taught from historical, linguistic, and social perspectives. Whatever drill that would be needed for students to learn the currently accepted rules could be integrated into a study of how rules and conventions arose, and of when they're useful and when they are used to sort people into inferior and superior groups.

I believe that students should learn the rules of spelling and grammar according to the *New York Times;* they should be able to read standard English and write in ways acceptable to current copyreaders and editors. However, they should also learn that rules are made by people and can be changed, broken, or discarded. They should also realize that language evolves and that it's necessary to know the rules if you intend to change or break them in a controlled way.

Language is a major resource, is empowering, but it is easy to forget that in classes where reading and writing are reduced to mechanical exercises and speech is impoverished or forbidden. In order to use the resources of language, one has to control it. For this reason one main focus of *Word Definitions of Experience* should be the development of the skill of questioning. Being able to ask questions makes it possible to take advantage of what other people know. There is skill involved in asking questions intelligently and being able to analyze answers. There is some truth in the cliché that a person gets what he or she asks for. I once worked with a group of twelve-year-olds on a project documenting the lives of their parents and grandparents. One of the girls had a great grandmother who was still alive. The girl discovered that her great grandmother lived through the San Francisco earthquake of 1906 and set up an interview so they could talk about what it was like during the Great Quake. The girl brought the tape of the interview to class and was reluctant to let us hear it. We finally persuaded her to play the tape and what we heard was:

GIRL: Granny, you were in the earthquake.
GRANNY: Yes.
GIRL: How was it?
GRANNY: Horrible.
GIRL: Thank you, Granny.

The girl was embarrassed. The problem she faced was not knowing how to ask questions and draw her granny out. Many of us don't know how to ask questions and regret not being able to draw people out and share in what they know and have experienced. School certainly doesn't help. Just about the only questions I remember asking in school from the first grade through junior high school were:

"Can I go to the bathroom?"
AND
"When is the assignment due?"

Question asking, that is, learning to use other people as resources, is a basic skill that should be encouraged and developed in every subject. Many questioning themes can be worked in, themes such as How do I ask questions about nature? (That is, how do I observe and design an experiment?)

- How can I ask someone to clarify the meaning of what they say or do?
- How do I ask for information from a stranger (e.g., how to get to a place, find out about the resources of a community, et cetera)?
- How do I approach people and find out about them when I'm in a new place?

Everyone at a school might even pause once a year and pose lists of questions to think about. This would be a sensible extension of the language program. Imagine asking fifty or a hundred young people to list questions they would like to see answered, posting the questions at the beginning of the school year, leaving them posted for several months, and then taking time to look at the questions again and discover whether anyone has found answers or tentative approximations to answers for some of the questions.

Language is a resource through books and other written matter as well as a bridge to other people's knowledge. Yet to know books, you must be surrounded by books. It is not enough to have textbooks and workbooks, or even a library you visit once a week. Books should be everywhere in any learning place, lots of books of different kinds. There should be student-made and -printed books, old books, picture books, books printed with different typefaces, books that express different opinions, books that raise questions, books that can transport students into worlds they have never seen or touched. The diversity of books is especially essential these days when large publishing houses are no longer committed to keeping books in print if they don't sell.

It's important to let students know that old books are not necessarily obsolete books, that answers to questions and needs can be found if you know how to search for books. I've found that one of the most useful skills one can have is *the skill of browsing,* of wandering through libraries, bookstores, subject index catalogs, *Books in Print,* in search of books that answer your needs. Research skills, that is, using books to get specific information, are extensions of the skills of browsing. They consist of knowing how to find and use books and involve more random search and intuitions than one would imagine. Contrary to the usual image of book research as looking up something in an encyclopedia, it can be a much more exciting adventure. If you have a subject to research, say, Napoleon, you can go to an encyclopedia. But you can also develop a series of associations with your subject and begin to piece together many different sources to develop a complex understanding of your subject. For

Napoleon, for example, here are some of the roads it might be interesting to follow:

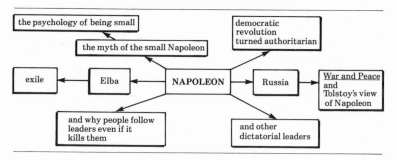

Research and browsing are skills that don't have to be taught separately. In a setting where questions are raised and students are encouraged to piece together answers from different sources, they are an integral part of everyday functioning.

There are some basic sources that every child should master, among them the etymological dictionary, the encyclopedia, and the library. In fact, once a child learned to read, say in the equivalent of the third grade where fluency usually develops, I would give him or her as a substitute for a report card a gift of an etymological dictionary, a one-volume encyclopedia, and a library card. This may sound strange but I know what the gift of a book can do. As a Jew, I was Bar Mitzvahed at thirteen, that is, officially taken into the community of adults. The symbol of that passage was a gift of my own prayer book. Even though I am not religious, the book is a symbol for me of being fully empowered.

Educational gifts are worth thinking about, especially if we are to welcome young people into our world and celebrate their growth. The idea of educational gifts for school children was developed by Friedrich Froebel, the originator of the kindergarten and a major influence on many American progressive educators. In the early nineteenth century, Froebel articulated a program for young children, which was designed to nurture growth through the orderly presentation of gifts.

The gifts have several purposes. One is to stimulate the child and provide play that leads toward physical and intellectual discovery. Another is to signify that a stage of growth has been passed through and that a new stage, incorporating the past and presenting new challenges, has been reached. Froebel's gifts are designed for children from birth to about six. It has occurred to me that some form of educational gifts might replace, in part, report cards and diplomas, and play the role of confirming progress and presenting new challenges throughout a young person's educational career. Gifts such as the etymological dictionary and miniencyclopedia I mentioned before could be supplemented by gifts of other educational tools that related directly to learning achieved. For example:

- upon completing their times tables, children could be given a slide rule with instructions on how it is constructed and how it could be used
- upon learning how to edit, layout, and design a small book, a gift of the University of Chicago *Manual of Style* can be made. Another gift could be a bound copy of each student's work
- upon learning how to repair a car or etch an electronic circuit board or build, wire, and plumb a small cabin, a kit of basic tools can be given to each pupil.

These gifts would provide students with mementos of their achievements and with tools to use for further learning. An A or B+ can provide some verification of learning, but it leads nowhere and leaves no specific memories. Gifts, tokens of welcome and future learning, can and might become symbols of achievement and tools for future growth. A series of educational gifts might provide young people with an educational toolbox they could use and expand throughout life.

Of course, these suggestions go beyond the language program and can be used in every area of study. There are gifts that can be worked into every aspect of a learning program. However, it is crucial not to confuse gifts with rewards. A gift is given to provide someone else with pleasure. It looks to the future and should be something that can be used. A reward is a token or memento of past performance more bound up with what has happened than with what can happen. All children should be given gifts as they move through different stages of development and these gifts should not be ranked or graded. There should be no A gifts, B gifts, or C, D, and E gifts, but equal tokens of our regard as adults and educators of our children's growth.

It is also possible to give group gifts, to provide young people with resources that extend their power and pleasure. One language resource I believe should be made available to all children is a *printing press*. The press is an instrument of freedom. Having access to a press and knowing how to use it makes it possible to get your words to others you will never see. It makes it possible on a modest level to give your views a chance in the world and to share your visions and experiences. The more presses we have, the more likely it is that people might come to know of each other. I believe that anyone who writes and wants to take a chance communicating through a book should have access to a press, to instructions on how to print, to information about the distributions of books, and to some paper and ink. This should be part of a language program, of *Word Definitions of Experience*, and not shunted off to a vocational education program. Certainly every child will not become a printer, but everyone ought to know how to print as much as how to write or type.

The history of printing and printing presses in American public schools provides an example of the way in which progressive innovations can be distorted or negated. As early as the 1870s, there was considerable controversy about the role of the textbook publishing industry in public education.

Colonel Francis Parker was one of the leading opponents of the use of standardized textbooks in the schools and gave speeches and wrote articles attacking the textbook companies. He proposed replacing all textbooks with a collection of library books and student- and teacher-written books. To facilitate the latter, he also proposed that schools have their own printshops, and that printing be taught as part of a comprehensive language arts program. When he became superintendent of schools in Quincy, Massachusetts, he implemented this idea throughout the system, and later, when he became head of the Cook County Normal School, he taught dozens of teachers the value of student-created and -published books.

The idea of printing as part of a comprehensive language program spread throughout the country in the early Progressive Education days, roughly from 1900 to the 1930s. However, the connection of printing with reading and writing gradually disappeared, especially with the emergence of a vocational education movement. Printing came to be looked on as a job, not as a tool for expression, as a part of a shop or vocational education program, not as an adjunct to the English or language arts program. By the time I was in junior high in 1951 to 1954, printing was required as a minor shop period and all we typeset and printed were business cards and letterheads. The only schoolwide uses of the presses (there were about ten small handpresses and one large motor-driven commercial press in the shop) were to print graduation programs, dance invitations, and report cards.

Still, the idea of having a press in every school as part of the language program is valid. I believe that writing is most effectively taught when one can see the best of one's work in print, and that taking part in the process of printing one's work can lead to greater affection for and care with the written word. For some students it can also open up the possibility of publishing books themselves. Every school should have a press and every student the opportunity to run some of his or her own work on it.

I am currently participating in an experiment involving ten schools, five of which recently purchased small printing presses. We gather once a month to produce a student-written, -managed, and -printed magazine. Students representing each school compose editorial boards that decide what gets published. Each editor is responsible for encouraging and editing the work in his or her school. We have a business board, a layout and design crew, and a printers guild. At the center of our work are those five presses. Printing is what makes the word live, is what gets it out in the community, is what makes writing more than an exercise for a grade. We have been able to make writing and printing major components of each school's language program.

Word Definitions of Experience should move from speech to print, encompass reading and writing, and focus on the meaning and content of human experience. In that way the first basic skill, the ability to use language well and thoughtfully, may be acquired.

BASIC SKILL 2:
The Ability to Think Through Problems and Experiment with Solutions

The ability to think does not develop spontaneously. Thought requires concentration, practice, and the ability to hold many things in one's mind at the same time. Though there may be some children born with exceptional powers of thought and concentration, these skills can also be developed and honed to a remarkable degree. It is possible to teach thinking skills, and it is essential for people who will be faced with choices and decisions all their lives to develop these skills as early and thoroughly as possible.

A separate subject entitled the *Development of Thinking Skills* should become a central part of young people's school experience. The subject would deal with three basic problems: confronting a new challenge, understanding something or someone who is *different,* and learning how to extract what is valuable in *old* forms. It would deal directly with *the basic skill of learning how to think.*

The *Development of Thinking Skills* would encompass the analysis of systems, the evaluation of alternate solutions to a problem, and the variety of techniques that can be used for organizing a body of information. It might deal with problems like:

- How can one find out what people think about a given question?
- What are ways of analyzing survey data and how reliable are these methods?
- What is the nature of predictions? What kind of information can lead to reliable predictions? What information doesn't lend itself to prediction at all?
- What is the nature of relationship? In space? Time? Between people? Between objects?
- What is the history of thought? How have different cultural traditions (and individuals) gone about defining and solving problems?
- How can numbers be used as a tool for organizing information?
- What is a system? How does one construct one?
- How are buildings, theories, books designed?

The goal of a series of classes on the *Development of Thinking Skills* is to show young people how to think through a problem, gather and organize information, and make hypotheses and draw conclusions about things in the world. It would be as much an integrative program as *Word Definitions of Experience.* It would encompass such subjects as logic, design, architecture, planning, systems analysis, art criticism, mathematics, writing, literary criticism, the history of technology and invention, the history of language and linguistics. The primary goals of the class (which could be

taught every year using different and increasingly sophisticated themes and techniques of analysis and criticism)
would be to give young people the power to plan a future,
to think through a problem, and to create solutions. The
class would be an attempt to counteract paralytic thinking
with active intelligence, to give young people the intellectual
tools necessary to live a decent life in a complex, often nasty,
world.

For young children the course can center on theses like:
How do people move water? How do you discover the
structure of an animal group? How do you fix a bicycle? How
do you put it together once you've taken it apart? How can
you plan in general to put something back together after
you've taken it apart?

For older students, problems can be more sophisticated.
For example, one course can center on the history of the
book. Who reads? Who controls publishing? How do books
get written? How do they get printed, distributed, adver-
tised? What goes into making a book a best seller? What goes
into preventing a book from reaching an audience? What is
censorship? How is the book industry organized? How does
one get enough information to answer these questions?

The subject would also have a personalized aspect. It
would help individual students learn how to organize working spaces for themselves, finding connections with their
own energy and style, and developing a resource library that
will be useful to them.

Some of the themes considered over the course of a person's time in school could be:

1. *Approaching new materials.* How to deal with the new,
either in terms of moving to a new community, or dealing
with a new job, or a new social or family problem, or a new
thing to learn.

2. *Figuring out what is wanted.* Understanding what is
expected before you decide to comply or not; how to get at
assumptions and make them fit in terms of mind, society,
politics, intellectual tradition, as well as how they relate to

your experience and how you can find ways to decide on how you feel and believe about them.

3. Uncovering contradictions. A valuable technique when dealing with any issue or topic or theory or experience is figuring out the contradictions inherent in it. Setting them side by side, solutions often emerge, or at least new directions of research or thought are indicated.

4. Formulations and reformulations. Ways of putting down initial ideas, and then organizing them. Writing with different colored pens, using a pair of scissors and a stapler; moving things around, eliminating them or developing new themes. This could also be called working habits.

BASIC SKILL 3:
The Ability to Understand Scientific and Technical Ideas and Use Tools

In addition to being able to use language well and to think, citizens of a democracy need to be able to understand, use, and control human inventions, from hammers to microcomputers. For this reason, the third strand of a reconstructed curriculum should deal with the subject of *Science, Technology, and the Use of Tools.*

School science tends to be twenty or more years behind current scientific practice, especially in the elementary and junior high schools. Part of the reason for this is that most teachers don't know science and depend upon whatever textbooks they have available; part is that science is not considered one of the "basics" and is usually placed just a cut above art and music in order of time priorities.

Technology fares even worse. There are usually a few lessons on the Industrial Revolution in fifth-grade history and perhaps in American and world history in high school, and possibly some atempts to introduce knowledge about the computer revolution as well.

There is no place in the present curriculum for considerations of how scientists and inventors work on an everyday level, or for serious consideration of issues like the social responsibility of science, the different social and political contexts in which technology and science can be used, whether "improvements" improve the quality of life, whether everyone benefits equally from science and technology, and whether the earth can survive their effects.

In addition, the use of tools of science and technology, from the hammer to the loom, lathe, computer, and electron microscope, are either not taught or are relegated to advanced science or vocational education.

Advanced science and vocational education: the two ends of the class system set up in school. Students are able to do one, not the other. Yet citizens of a democracy, people who have power over their lives, should be able to use both computers and hammers. Manual labor and intellectual labor are not incompatible. Moreover, people should have knowledge of how everyday things work and can be constructed, repaired, and improved, as well as professional knowledge. It is important for children of carpenters and children of computer experts to know how to use hammers and computers, to know how to organize information about how a house can be built or repaired, and about how a computer can be used to control inventory of a small business or large corporation. That doesn't mean that everyone will end up being either a carpenter or computer expert or both, but that people who work will be able to respect each other and that our children will be taught how to work with their heads and their hands.

There are a number of implications in considering science, technology, and the use of tools to be basic skills. One is that scientists in the schools, machinists in the schools, inventors in the schools, should be as common as artists in the schools. We simply cannot depend upon teachers to provide adequate information and current means of using the information. We should draw on the people who do the work, and it should be their obligation (as well as a possible source of renewal for them) to offer what they know to young people.

Teachers can, however, help provide history, analyze the political and social roles of science and technology, supervise student projects, et cetera. However, this would require knowledgeable teachers, people who will work at their profession and not be bound to textbooks or what they learned at teachers college. Technology moves fast, scientists disagree, and new discoveries are overthrowing old theories all the time. Teachers cannot be expected to know everything about their subjects but they should be literate and current. I have known science teachers who can't follow an article in *Scientific American;* schools where minicomputers sit in a closet because the teachers don't know how to use them; and worse, many, many students who will never see a computer, run a lathe, machine a screw, handle a press, try out a loom, look through a microscope. Science and technology will be mysteries to them, though some will learn to use hand tools and repair machines at home despite school.

We have to empower young people through command of science, technology, and the use of tools; through an understanding of technical information and the strategies used (mostly mathematical) to organize it and develop applications. We must also not leave out in the process consideration of whom science and technology serves, for it can be used to serve democracy or to crush it. *Science, Technology, and the Use of Tools* would deal with units like the following:

1. *Engines and motors:* Their development, their use and repair, their manufacture, the positive and negative effects of their use, smog and the internal combustion engine, the tools needed to make and repair an engine, and so on.

2. *Weaving:* The role of clothes in history, the cottage industry and the development of large-scale weaving, weavers and unionizations, the technical history of the loom, the biological nature of fibers, plastics and weaving, portraits of a Rochdale weaving cooperative and the J. P. Stevens Corporation, the practice of weaving and the design of fabrics and cloth.

3. *The history of joining things together:* Hammers, nails,

screws, bolts, fasteners, and the development of bridges and airplanes.

4. *Cutting:* The social and practical history of knives and saws, from the stone blade to the logging chain saw, including the use and sharpening of saws, the effects of the logging industry; the development of the laser and of electronic processes for fine cutting; diamond cutting and the agony in the diamond mines of South Africa; cutting coal and the life of a coal miner; cutting stone, and the Pyramids and who built them.

5. *Machines that make machines and men and women who invent machines:* On the development of the tool-and-die industry, practice making tools and creating tools to solve physical problems, and so forth.

6. *Computing and computing devices, from the abacus to the home computer:* With a study of miniaturization and its role in developing the power of computers, as well as a study in the use of base-two number systems, an introduction to data processing, to BASIC and other computer languages, to the limits of computer-stored information; the social history of IBM, as well as the effect of computers on working-class people, et cetera.

7. *Clones:* The study of cellular life, the story of the discovery of DNA, the building of models of DNA, the social dangers of cloning, the definition and understanding of macro- and microbiological levels, with discussion and demonstration of mutations, using electron microscopes, studying and cultivating bacteria, et cetera.

These seven units are just some of hundreds that could be developed. Other illustrations of the range of what could be taught are:

1. model making, plastic and mathematical
2. surveys and the use of numbers to organize information
3. agriculture: how to plant and how to maintain the productivity of the earth

4. the building of Chartres Cathedral compared with the building of the Seagram's Building.

All of these classes would involve technical knowledge, practice in gathering and organizing information, and using tools. They would also deal with social, economic, cultural, and political aspects of science and technology; with history and perhaps most importantly with speculation about the role science, technology, and tools can play in a democracy. Ecological and environmental considerations would not be secondary but, to use a term from weaving, built into the very fabric of learning. The human and earth dimensions of science and technology would not be separated as they currently are, nor would the lines between the technical, artistic, and social worlds.

It may be objected that this is a lot to expect young people to be able to master. I'm not sure; no one knows how much and on what level of sophistication children can learn. The limitations on school learning that are imposed upon most children come from teachers' lack of knowledge, contentless curricula, limited resources, foolish organizational structures, and fear of democracy, not from anything having to do with young people or their capabilities.

Interesting lessons in science, technology, and tools can be done on a classroom and individual level. Nevertheless, many scientific and technical resources as well as tools are expensive and are also beyond what any single classroom or teacher can be expected to provide. Centers for the study of science, technology, and the use of tools should be established throughout the country and be made available to all children.

These centers should be joined with centers of the arts and form seminal places of learning in the community. There is no reason to separate science and the arts. In fact, there are many reasons to combine them and give all children access to technology as well as to arts. The study of computers can encompass graphics as well as programming; the study of printing fits well with the creation of literature, just as painting, and dying cloth fit with the physics of color. Centers for arts and sciences should be established throughout the country, giving arts and sciences equal status, since the ability to participate in and enjoy the arts is a fourth basic skill.

BASIC SKILL 4:
The Ability to Use the Imagination and to Participate in and Appreciate Personal and Group Expression

Painting, drawing, music, film, dance, video, poetry, theater, and other forms of personal and group expression are basic to the development of articulate individuals and cohesive groups. As John Dewey said in 1914,

> Viewed both psychologically and socially, the arts represent not luxuries and superfluities but *fundamental forces of development*.[35]

Experience with art leads to the development of the imagination, to the playful exercise of the mind that leads to the solution of social and technical as well as artistic problems.

The development of imagination is a basic skill. The attempt to express feelings or ideas through art is essential for coming to terms with experience. People come to know themselves and others better through song, dance, and theater. They learn ways of organizing the visual world through painting, drawing, video, and film. All the arts provide ways of experimenting with the possible, of extending oneself and participating with others in fulfilling collective activity. Theater, for example, makes it possible for people to play at being others and become involved in complex, often painful, situations while staying safe. Theatrical distance allows people to rehearse action, a privilege we are

not often afforded in everyday life. The visual arts can represent reality, fantasy, or even pure form. They teach control
and thought. Classes in life drawing, in perspective, or in
abstract painting provide as many useful techniques for
organizing information as classes in arithmetic and social
studies.

The idea that arts are frills and privileges and not basics
is a manifestation of the antidemocratic sentiment that is
current in politics. It is a way of saying that the development of the imagination and the pleasures provided by the
arts should be luxuries; and that children must be born into
families with money in order to learn music, drawing, dance,
filmmaking, video.

It is a way of putting a price on the quality of life and the
ability to use the imagination. I feel that some of the recent
attempts, in the service of so-called back-to-basics movements, to cut art programs from public schools really mask
a desire to see that poor people's children are denied the
educational opportunities of the more advantaged. Certainly
it would be difficult to argue that plane geometry is more
basic or useful in adult life than the ability to play the piano
or sketch a face.

The relegation of the arts to frills or minor subjects reminds me of a recent controversy over housing for the poor
in New York City. A group of architects and community
people planned and built an elegant, well-designed housing
development for low-income families on 101 and 102 streets
on the East Side of New York. The cost was within the usual
guidelines for low-income housing, though the apartments
were spacious. There were terraces, space reserved for community gardens, well-lit hallways, recreation centers. In fact,
they looked like well-planned condominiums of the sort that
are usually considered luxury apartments. A great uproar developed, caused most likely by the construction and real
estate industries, over opening the project. The overt argument was that the poor don't deserve such beautiful housing.

The covert consideration was that if the poor could live well cheaply, then the price of housing for the wealthy would be driven down.

I sense the same undemocratic sentiment behind the ruthless cuts of art programs going on now. Communities that have resources raise money to keep their programs going, and the children of all the rest of the people have to fend as best they can.

The arts are basic, and the creative use of the imagination is a basic skill. Schools should have arts programs that are given the same priorities as language and technology. All of these programs should concentrate on developing the creative capacities of children and helping them learn to analyze experience and solve problems. In the arts classes, these should be available to all students:

Drawing, Sketching, and Thinking with a Pencil, a program stretching over several years, encompassing, among other things, life drawing, architectural drawing, the use of thumbnail sketches and other drawing techniques to visualize solutions to problems, technical and scientific drawing, the drawing of faces throughout history, the rendering of human and animal expression, and the explanation of media for drawing, from pen, pencil, and charcoal to computer graphics.

Another art strand could deal with *filmmaking,* ranging from simple stop-action animation, to studying editing techniques, sound synchronization, storyboarding and scriptwriting, studying the history of film, and analyzing current films.

Theater could be taught and be a supplement to the classes on *Word Definitions of Experience.* Students could learn acting, scene construction, the history of theatrical makeup and costume, playwriting. Six plays dealing with family tragedy from Sophocles to Edward Albee could be studied and performed, or themes such as unrequited love, defiance of authority, or possession could be studied through playreading and performance.

The possibilities of developing art curricula have hardly been explored. By considering the arts to be frills, current educators have often turned their programs into frilly, superficial attempts at self-expression.

Decent programs should incorporate history, technique, performance, and practice, as well as the technical aspects of the art and criticism.

There have been a number of attempts to deal with the arts as basic skills. They have worked admirably both in terms of developing students' imaginative and artistic abilities and in improving other skills (such as reading and writing) that are used within the arts programs. Colonel Francis Parker's school, the Cook County Normal School, is one example and there are many more examples from the twenties and thirties. Some of these schools have been described in detail. It is worth looking back to what was done by Marrietta Johnsen in Stanhope, Alabama, by the Walden School and the New Lincoln School, as well as by Sybil Marshall in England.[36]

One recent example of a comprehensive basic skill arts program within a public school is the Teachers and Writers Collaborative program at P.S. 75 Manhattan. P.S. 75 has for the last nine years been the central focus for the work of the Teachers and Writers Collaborative. The relationship between P.S. 75 and Teachers and Writers began when Lou Mercado, the principal, volunteered to have his school participate in the collaborative's Writers-in-the-Schools program. Phillip Lopate was the writer chosen by the collaborative, and the story of his first years at 75 was described in his marvelous book *Being with Children*. Over the years Lopate was joined by other artists, and they developed artist teams that worked in the school with teachers and directly with students. The curriculum centered about writing and printing books and comics, filmmaking, radio, drama, painting and drawing, theater, videodrama. All these means of personal and group expression were centered on the content of life. Children created stories and plays and films of their own. But they also performed Chekhov and studied the history of film. The collaborative, with the help of the staff of 75, created what Lopate calls a laboratory of art at the school. The work of the students required considerable discipline and study. What is unique about the work at P.S. 75 is that it did not merely involve students "expressing themselves" but involved history, technique, technology — many different studies more demanding than anything found in workbooks and textbooks. Student expression developed within the context of rich, demanding study.

I have found that many people confuse an educational program that considers expression basic, with the idea that all children's expression in its raw and undisciplined form is wonderful. This view leads to no growth. Children develop their means of expression through training, observation, and practice, through studying the history of art and knowing what other people have done and are doing, through making mistakes and producing many bad, uninspired works as well as occasionally achieving excellence. A program that includes classes in life drawing, the history of sculpture, music performance in different cultural traditions, the revision of fiction, poetic composition, Greek theater, should not be confused with one that gives children paper, pencil, and paints, and lets them "express themselves."

I have directed performances of *Antigone* and *A Midsummer Night's Dream* with seven- to thirteen-year-olds, have discussed Shakespeare with children as young as seven, have worked on productions of *The Doll's House* and *Golden Boy* with fifth, sixth, and seventh graders. The children were interested in these works because Antigone is about female defiance of male royal authority, because *A Midsummer Night's Dream* is about magic and love triangles, because Shakespeare deals with murder and love, because he can be raucously funny and delicately romantic, because in other words, the stuff of great expressive works is the content of life. Content is the core of significant, motivated learning, and some major ways of organizing and understanding this content are what we call artistic. Art, the many forms of personal and group expression, should be a major aspect of a reconstructed basic-skills curriculum.

Resources must be allocated so that students have opportunities to experience and participate in music, dance, the visual arts, theater. It is foolish to try to do this on a classroom level, for no teacher can be expected to be competent or even knowledgeable in all the arts, just as no teacher can command all of science and technology. Nor can every classroom be a theater, dance studio, art workshop, poetry center, or film lab. Art centers have to be created that are staffed by artists and teachers that serve all the schools. These centers could be attached to school systems or they could serve multiple purposes, such as providing working space for artists, community arts programs, and exhibits and performances. I've mentioned this to a number of people who have pointed out to me that there isn't money these days for such ambitious building plans and for additional salaries. My response is that athletic complexes continue to be built and maintained, that competitive sports are supported in a way that makes them as functionally basic to American education as reading or arithmetic and perhaps more basic than writing. If we were committed to supporting the arts in the same way, we would allocate community resources to building and maintaining art centers, which could also serve as science, technology, and tool centers. At first, local efforts will be crucial. Donated land, a rented storefront, a reconstructed empty supermarket would do. Everything from bake sales to foundation proposals should be explored and community energy should be mobilized the way in which it can be mobilized to support a football team or a cheerleading squad.

It is important to stop thinking of the classroom as the basic unit of instruction. There is no reason why students of all ages couldn't spend a quarter to a half of their time at an art center or, for that matter, why classes in history, math, science, English, and so on, couldn't take advantage of such a center to enrich the content of what is being explored in those classes.

A *center of expression* could contain, in addition to space for dance, theater, and music, collections of historical documents, photos, slides, and recordings. It could be a place where the expressive forms of the peoples of the earth can be reproduced, compared, and used as resources to nurture the imagination of young people.

The center could also contain students' work, the work of contemporary artists, community history, photo collections. It could be a source for community renewal. What is crucial, though, is that centers of expression be staffed by practicing artists as well as teachers and archivists. The expressive arts cannot merely be left to educators without becoming stale, textbook imitations of art. New people, actively involved in creative work, need to be brought into the world of schools, new credentials created if necessary. I'm tired of seeing qualified artists, musicians, and writers involved in artists-in-the-schools programs being forced to work with bored teachers because state laws say that students can't be left without credentialed supervisors in public schools. It's silly, negative, and expensive.

BASIC SKILL 5:
The Ability to Understand How People Function in Groups

Knowing about others, about people in groups, is basic to understanding the rewards and responsibilities of citizenship in a democracy, and there should be a subject studied throughout a student's school years called *People in Groups.*

Groups can be looked at from many perspectives. They can be examined politically, that is, from the perspective of how power functions in the group

- economically, according to the distribution of wealth and work within the group

- historically, as the development of the group over time
- socially, according to relations of caste, class, and kinship
- culturally, according to style, habit, custom, and patterned relationship among individuals or groups.

In current school practice these subjects are covered in social studies in the early grades and in history and geography in the upper grades. The amount of information provided students is meager. Yet, in order to become a responsible and intelligent citizen in a complex pluralistic democracy like ours, there is an enormous amount of political, social, cultural, historical, and economic information people must absorb and analyze. On a minimal level, young people should learn:

1. How to understand cultural differences without using words like "primitive," "dirty," "deficient." Cultural ignorance is at the base of much racism and conflict. Recently I heard a dramatic instance of this from some people who were studying racial conflict in the United States Army. It seems that many white officers interpreted certain forms of greeting, walking, and dressing that are signs of friendship and respect in black communities as defiance and disrespect. This misinterpretation led to black enlisted men being disciplined for what they perceived as positive gestures. The only sensible interpretation the black soldiers could make of the white officers' actions was that they were racist.

The same racial misunderstanding and fear exist in school between student groups, and students and teachers. Simple-seeming things like eye contact, handshakes, style of dress, tone of voice, display of hostility and affection differ from group to group, and these differences often lead to misunderstanding and, at worst, violence.

Culture should be studied explicitly in order to give young people a sense of the variety of ways people approach social interaction and organization. They should also be given techniques for observing others without judging them, and for building a picture of a culture that differs from their own. I believe the knowledge of one's own and other people's culture is basic to democratic education and think that the graduation requirement at the Open School in St. Paul, Minnesota, that students "demonstrate an understanding of the difference in attitude, actions, and experience of one's own culture and at least two others, one of which must be Spanish-speaking American, Native American, or Black American," should be part of everyone's schooling.

2. *How politics works, who has power and how it is used.* This is a survival course. Young people have to know how to trace the sources of power, understand indirect manipulation, coercion, seduction, and other forms of control, if they themselves are to take power over their own lives. Looking for where the power is, going directly to the center of power if you want something, developing alternate sources of power, and even knowing something about oppressing those in power are important. Over the past years we have been victimized by abuses of power again and again, have been deceived by leaders, and by control of information, by false words, and we should not wish our children to be as stupid as we have been. Politics, as I conceive of it, is not simply the study of politicians and government. In some societies power and government may be identical. That is not the case in our society, and the complex interplay of many sectors, each with differing power, determines the character of society more than government does. Of course, once one starts studying politics in this broader sense, one realizes how difficult it is to get information about the sources of power and the relations of power blocs to each other and to the people they supposedly serve. However, the attempt to acquire information about power and to organize the fragments one can obtain, will itself be a basic education on the power of information.

3. *How to gather historical information.* Primary sources should be used wherever possible: people should be heard in their own voices. In addition, the idea that some people, the "civilized" ones, have history and that other people don't

should be dispelled. All peoples have history, and so far as I know, all peoples have recorded some of that history, whether through myth, song, oral poetry, or through writing. Moreover, all peoples have ways of interpreting their own history, and it is important to understand that if we are to make any sense of some of the major problems in the world. Language and civil wars, border disputes, alliances and enmities take on their particular characters because of people's interpretation of their own history. A more sophisticated understanding, for example, of the complex perceptions of Asian history that differ from nation to nation and ethnic group to ethnic group might have saved us a lot of grief in the sixties and seventies. The same could be said of our blundering in Iran.

4. *That social relations have their history and are part of culture.* However, they can also be looked at separately, and such topics as family structure, the anatomy of friendship, courtship and marriage, the development of fraternal and sororal associations, clubs, and clans can illuminate history and culture. They can also lead to insight about the behavior of people who are culturally different. In some cultures, for example, a child's mother's brother is as central in the child's life as is the father. In others a grandmother is the central figure. I've seen instances where an insult to a grandmother led to serious fights, and others where a sensible appeal to the correct uncle overcame serious discipline problems.

These days when there is much talk about the sanctity of the family, the collapse of the family, the development of alternate families, the demise of the nuclear family, the rise of communal families, and so on, it would be sensible to study family and small group structures and provide young people with information of the range of kinship structures that people have invented.

5. *That economics in its broadest sense is perhaps the most neglected basic.* Teachers tend to avoid discussing topics like the distribution of wealth, the effects of poverty,

the struggles to achieve economic equality, class conflict and class interest, the range of economic organizations, from capitalist to socialist and communist, the effects of economic interest on politics, the relationship between capitalism and democracy, et cetera. Economic information is withheld and, as adults, people listen passively and dispiritedly while words such as *depression, recession,* and *inflation* are used to conceal different forms of economic manipulation. A good example of the distortion economic ignorance creates is the current fad called cultural journalism as embodied by *Foxfire* magazine and the Foxfire books. Cultural journalism is fairly widespread. It consists of having elementary or high school students interview older people and document their way of life. Because of the way questions are asked in most cultural journalism projects, the results turn out to portray the "good old days" when life was simple and folks were happy doing crafts and hunting and growing their own food. Perusing the many publications of cultural journalism, one find articles on poultices but not on poverty, on yokes but no unions, on stump waters but not on strikes. The overall picture presented of poor people is of good ingenious folk who have preserved traditional ways of doing things. There is hardly a mention that the ingenuity of poor folk was a product of their poverty and that poverty is painful, not quaint. There are no rich people indifferent to the poor, there is no class conflict, labor struggle, or exploitation. The picture is pretty and millions of copies of books on the old-time crafts sit on coffee tables throughout the country. Yet from my perspective, the picture they present of life is not merely selective but actually an insult to the dignity and struggles of poor people.

This points to a basic concern that a reconstructed education must have. Life in groups must be examined from at least four different perspectives if we are to provide young people with adequate information to form a just picture of how people live. The study of *People in Groups* would examine group life from *political, cultural, social-historical,* and *economic* perspectives. There are different ways the subject could be organized. For example, a year could be devoted to studying one's local community from those perspectives, another to studying a series of events, like the Revolutionary or Civil War, from those perspectives. One could look at the lives of United States Presidents from historical, political, economic, social, and cultural perspectives, or examine the armed forces. Other nations and cultures could be examined, and perhaps, after a while, classes in gathering and organizing information from different perspectives can be offered. One can take documents like the United States Constitution and ask what social, political, economic, cultural, and historic factors contributed to its construction.

The study of *People in Groups* could also deal directly with democratic values and how they have appeared and disappeared over time, and how they have manifested themselves in different systems. The relation between the study of *People in Groups* and an adequate understanding of democracy should make it basic in a public school curriculum.

In addition, the resources that exist within one's own community should be incorporated into the study of people. Schools should be places where peoples of different cultural backgrounds can meet respectfully and share their strengths. Cultural resources are fundamentally people resources. Older people, the bearers and recorders of cultural history, ought to be welcomed and invited. Schools can make attempts to document the history of their communities; to compose, print, record, and illustrate aspects of the culture and history of the people they serve. Every school should have an archive of photos, tapes, booklets, interviews so they develop a past and a character that can be known to everyone in the community. The *People in Groups* class could coordinate this archive, which would be one way a school could define and celebrate its uniqueness. As a bonus, such an archive would help new teachers who are not from the community learn about the people they have been hired to serve.

The notion of community needn't be interpreted narrowly and confined to a few blocks, a part of a city, or even a county. A learning program cañ build in student mobility. Students could have a chance to touch rural and urban environments, to spend time (on exchange programs or overnights) with people unlike themselves. It is important to help young people experience the marvelous complexity of our nation so they can learn not to be afraid of diversity. They should understand the joys and sorrows of different peoples, see land that has been devastated and land that has been nurtured, see rewarding work and hard, unrewarding labor. In particular, this might mean that the study of *People in Groups* might also involve

- pairing urban and rural schools and exchanging visits
- having children go to work with their parents and other people's parents
- having two teachers work together, an inside teacher and an outside teacher, one who travels away from the central learning place with some children while the other works with the rest of the children
- setting up apprenticeships and learning so that (for older children) about half the students are out working and learning in the community at any time
- developing long-range exchanges of students from all schools similar to those supported by the National Association of Independent Schools. (The association identifies high schools that have special learning programs, such as in music, marine biology, theater, or filmmaking. It then coordinates year-long student exchanges among those high schools.)

BASIC SKILL 6:
Learning How to Learn Throughout Life and to Contribute to the Nurturance of Others

We all run down occasionally, get weary of the daily round, and need sources of renewed strength and learning.

As individuals we need to continue learning new things to stay fresh. We need times to play and forget the stresses of our usual lives. We also need the renewal provided by passing on what we know to others, and by serving our communities. In addition to learning, play, teaching, and service, we have to contribute to the renewal of the earth, which is our major resource and the source of our lives. We become strong by giving as well as taking and consuming. Ecology, environmental action, and the recycling of resources is both an obligation of being a citizen of the earth and a source of personal renewal.

The basic skills, though acquired and practiced through school, are basic because of the power they provide us as adults. Young people need to understand this and know that what they are learning will be useful and empowering throughout life. They also need to anticipate the need for renewal and to understand that learning is not merely a school matter, but a source of growth and vitality throughout life. There are a number of ways techniques for personal and group renewal can be part of a learning program devoted to keeping language, imagination, invention, thought, and sensitivity basic throughout life. Here are some of them that could be organized through a subject called *Learning to Learn and Teach.*

Renewal through Lifelong Learning
If one identified learning with school-learning, it would be difficult to make a case for the notion that lifelong learning can be a source of renewal. Who would want to go to school all one's life? Luckily school-learning is a small part of what one learns and it often doesn't prevent us from learning new skills, crafts, arts, concepts, and ideas throughout life. Ronald Gross, in his book *The Lifelong Learner*, defines lifelong learners as people who recognize some of the following characteristics in themselves:

- You are open to new experiences, ideas, information, and insights.
- You like to make things happen instead of waiting for life to act on you.
- There are always things you'd love to know more about, appreciate better, or learn to do. In fact, you never have the feeling that you know everything, have every skill, you'll ever need to know.
- You feel better about yourself when you are successfully learning something new.
- You've learned enormously from certain important experiences which don't usually rate as "subjects."
- You often learn a great deal in ways other than taking courses.
- The kind of life you want to lead five years from now requires that you begin to learn new things now.
- You believe that investing in your own growth is the best investment in your future — occupational or personal.
- You have been attracted by, or perhaps are already enrolled in, one of the new kinds of educational programs for adults offered by colleges and universities around the country.[37]

Ron Gross's book is addressed to people out of school. In a decent school situation learning would not take any single form, nor would it be boring or excessively mechanical. It would be an extension of life outside of school and pass naturally into life after school. Lifelong learning would be constantly referred to, and perhaps every topic studied or class taken would end not with a grade, but with a personal evaluation and a series of suggestions of how what has been learned could be expanded on and how students can pursue additional learning themselves. The purpose of taking time to suggest ways students can continue to learn on their own and initiate new learning is not to encourage students to act immediately. It is a way of giving them strengths for the future, when they might become bored with what they're doing, tired of old ways, and hungry for some new content in their lives. It is not the specific suggestions that are important so much as the constant reminder that it is always possible to learn. Teachers in all subjects should leave their students with a sense

- of where they can go to learn more about a subject
- of what techniques are valuable for self-teaching (which is not the same as having good study skills in school)
- that it's never too late to pursue a subject or learn something new
- that it's perfectly all right to learn something because you care to even if you may never use it.

Lifelong learning doesn't have to be an individual activity. There are times, especially as one grows older, when community and culture are important, and learning and working cooperatively with others is a source of renewing personal energy. An account of adult learning in community is provided by Enok Mortensen talking of his first experiences participating in folk schools.

The word *folk* in the term folk schools does not have the same meaning as *folk* in English, where the term is associated with folk music and quaint, but naive, arts and crafts. Folk is used in the Danish sense of *volk*, people. A folk school is a people school; a place where people came together to celebrate and preserve their culture and to share their knowledge of the world around them.

There were a few students and only a couple of teachers, but they all spoke Danish, and never had it been so wonderful to get up in the morning anticipating new experiences and discoveries. The day began with breakfast and morning devotion. We sang familiar and beloved songs. Then there were classes. Ragnhild Strandskov taught music, Danish and physical education. . . .

Alfred C. Nielsen lectured on social problems and literature. He gave me special instruction in English, and in addition to acquiring the rudiments of English grammar I discovered the vast world of literature. We read poetry as well as contemporary novels. I learned of Sinclair Lewis and Willa

Cather and I became acquainted with the sophisticated *American Mercury* and the nihilistic Mencken. In the most Danish of all atmospheres my horizons were widened, and I was well on the way toward becoming an American. . . .

That summer passed all too quickly, but for me it was a rejuvenating experience, listening and learning. From one point of view it was like coming home to find half-forgotten values, and I cherished the cozy little world of the school, a close knit community of kindred souls; but paradoxically the world also widened and became larger as I sensed new goals and purpose for my life.[38]

In the past there were many different kinds of schools adults set up in order to teach each other and learn together. These schools didn't need to have grades and report cards, or to separate different areas of learning. Reading and writing were important but so was singing, dancing, building, creative art. Most important perhaps was talking and being together. These schools ranged from labor schools to settlement-house schools, took place in apartments, in churches, in the backs of stores. They existed because they gave the learners power, joy, and comradeships.

Young people need to learn how to initiate and conduct classes if they are to bring people together for purposes of learning as adults. Every school should provide for student-taught and -initiated classes. They could range from a simple fifteen-minute class on how to do magic tricks, to classes on particular books, to classes on computers, or on music, or motorcycle repair. The sum of what is known by all the people in a group should be the strength of the whole group. There does not have to be one teacher and many students. Even five-year-olds have things to teach, and the sooner they learn that what they know can be of value to others, and that others can also offer them something valuable, the quicker respect and the pleasures of being part of a community will grow.

Play as a Source of Renewal

Some scholars and students of play have asserted that play is serious business. I'd like to take an opposite position and assert that play is that part of life that is deliberately not serious. When games become professional or too emotional, play becomes life; the pleasure of participation turns into the grief of defeat and the gloating of victory.

This is particularly true of child's play, which can easily be overinterpreted and can be turned from pleasurable activity to performance for adult approval.

A good example of contrasting ways of understanding play is the attitudes toward long-distance running held by African and American athletes. Of course there are exceptions. Americans run seriously and feel terrible when they lose. They are condescending toward the losers when they win. The crucial thing for many African runners is a good race. If you win by such a large margin that there was no race at all, you've lost the pleasure of racing. A race needs winners and losers and they need each other in order to have a good race. Therefore, winners and losers respect and congratulate each other for the pleasure of racing they have provided each other. The same is true of a game of basketball, football, and even chess, or Go. Winning by fifty points or in ten moves is no fun, no game.

The essence of competitive *play* is a well-played game in which the contestants respect and challenge each other and the goal is pleasure, not merely victory.[39]

The concept of well-played games should be integrated into the games children play, not merely for the pleasure it can provide in their immediate lives but also because playing well and for pleasure can be a constant source of renewal all of our lives.

Handicapping systems often help to make games equal. Constant shifting of sides, games with no score kept, games where the rules change every time they're played, should all be experimented with. Physical activity, both for individuals and groups, has to be a part not merely of school life but of adult life as well or we shrivel up. Play in the larger sense, that is, activity without judgment or consequence, is necessary for survival. We need a time free of the stress of competition in our adult lives in order to renew our energy to face the pressures of living. And we need to learn young how to take this time. I find it distressing that in most schools play is turned into bitter competition; the pleasure of participating turned into the pressure of performing.

Play should be a basic part of the curriculum, and playing well, rather than winning, should be the goal. This means that young people should be taught a wide variety of field and board games, exposed to dozens of different kinds of exercises, and given the opportunity to organize and create their own games. They should also be introduced to non-competitive games and understand that playing does not always involve competition.

One of the most important consequences of teaching play might turn out to be giving young people opportunities to organize themselves to participate in group activities that provide them with pleasure. I've been quite distressed recently talking to bored youngsters between the ages of ten and sixteen. They complain that there's nothing to do and often get in trouble doing nothing. They tell me they are waiting for some adult to come along and organize a game or a tournament or a community center, and when I suggest they do it themselves, they shrug and close up. If there is any comment it's usually, "We're kids, we can't do anything." That attitude doesn't provide one with much positive feeling about the future of our democracy.

Renewal through Teaching and Service

Helping others get strong and learn new things can be a source of personal energy. It is a matter of one's attitude toward the learner or the person that is served. It's interesting to take an inventory of all the people in a community who choose to teach for their pleasure and not as a job. In our small community there are Little League and basketball coaches; people who teach knitting and crocheting, weaving, computer programming, and writing on an informal level. There are several men's and women's groups where people try to teach each other how to cope with personal stress. In addition, there are Boy Scouts, Cub Scouts, Brownies and Girl Scouts, and the 4-H Club. I, personally, have been taught how to use a chain saw, to recognize and collect good firewood, and to repair roofs, among other things, by neighbors. In exchange I have offered to teach people how to use our letterpress, how to write, and how to help their children read and write. Sharing one's skills and being involved in a community where certain skills and services are part of a natural round of exchanges provides one with a sense of participation, of belonging somewhere. The use and exchange of skills other than in the service of making money is a binding force in the development of decent community. It is important for children to understand that teaching, that sharing what one knows, is a potential source of personal strength and friendship and not merely a loss of competitive advantage.

It is also important for them to learn the difference between charity and service. Charity consists of taking a little time to give something you can do without to people in need. Charity does not deal with the fundamental problem of empowering the needy or of changing the competitive nature of society, which creates an unbalanced distribution of resources that leads to poverty and disability. Service is different from charity. It is an empowering activity and its goal is to enable those served to become strong enough to lead full lives and offer services in exchange. In my experience, no one wants to be helped without returning a service, and if you know and value people's strengths it is unlikely that an occasion for the return of a favor will not arise. All you have to do is ask for help. Asking for help is the other face of teaching and providing services to others. Unfortunately, many people are too shy or too proud to ask for help. It is considered bad manners: an internalization, I suppose, of the competitive ideology of our society, where the strong win and weakness is a sign of deserved inferiority.

Young people are not encouraged to ask for help and in highly competitive classrooms are simply afraid to show their ignorance. I remember observing a second grader who transferred into my class during his first week. It was clear he didn't understand what we were studying and I waited the first week hoping he'd ask for help. By Friday he was not merely confused but angry, a budding discipline problem. I finally took him aside and asked him if he was confused. He denied it but I went ahead and explained things to him anyway. After an hour together he thanked me for the help. I finally asked him why he didn't ask me or one of the other students for help before. His answer was that you're not supposed to ask for help in school because then the teacher will know what you don't know and give you a bad grade and the other children will think you're dumb.

We have to share what we know, in the classroom and in our adult lives. I believe students should become accustomed to teaching others as well as asking for help from students and teachers. Asking for and offering help should be a part of school life from a child's earliest days. In addition, children should have occasion to serve the whole school and the community at large. This can mean anything from cleaning up a dirty lot and turning it into a garden or park, to making regular visits to people who are not mobile and cooking, cleaning, shopping, and reading for them. Perhaps the class on *Learning to Learn and Teach* or a part of the class should be devoted each year to the subject of how to serve others and the community. This class could deal with themes like:

- identifying community problems
- developing strategies for solving problems
- organizing others to help you
- helping people without insulting them
- helping people acquire the power to help themselves
- styles of teaching and styles of learning
- what trust in your student means
- devising new teaching methods
- designing solutions to an educational problem.

It is not far-fetched to imagine that a group of six-year-olds can spend a half hour a day for several weeks studying the various ways in which people have tried to teach reading and trying the methods out on each other. Nor is it impossible for junior and high school students to mobilize themselves to build a greenhouse and maintain a garden or assume the responsibility for the safety of older people on the streets in communities where police protection is inadequate. Moreover, learning to act for others provides a confirmation of one's own strength that can renew a commitment to live decently and vigorously at times when one is tired of the competitive grind all of us are exposed to no matter what our intents.

Renewal and the Earth

I have seen a number of school recycling programs begin with enthusiasm and then fade out. Collecting cans, bottles, and papers can become boring however sensible and necessary it is. It is a bit like washing dishes. We all know that it is a futile cyclic activity because the dishes will become dirty again. The reason most of us manage to clean the dishes most of the time is that we have to eat, can't afford new dishes every meal, and are not particularly inclined to eat off dirty dishes on the table. The consequences of not recycling materials or taking better care of the earth are not so immediate, nor do we see the larger consequences of our personal waste and carelessness. When people toss a beer can out of the window of their car or leave a beach littered, they don't think in terms of 100 million beer cans and square miles of plastic wrappings. But that is the magnitude of the problem: the tons and miles of waste and a geologic environment unable to produce new resources at the same rate as they are being depleted.

The habit of linking individual actions to consequences within groups and on the scale of the earth has to be developed if we are to have much of an earth left to pass on to our grandchildren and their grandchildren. Sometimes we have to think over generations and not just of ourselves and our children. Contributing to the maintenance and renewal of the earth may not lead to immediate pleasures and might even cause inconvenience as we cut down on the things we own and the energy we consume. Yet there is a global pleasure that it is possible to experience, what could be called metaphysical or spiritual pleasure, from contributing to the maintenance of the earth and being a positive part of a whole of which your own life and actions are an insignificant part. That pleasure is a source of renewal, a small affirmation that we are trying to live decently and respect the whole.

It would be a good idea to devote time through integrated study in the rest of the curriculum to study cycles and systems. The study would consist of consideration of:

- life cycles
- geological cycles
- the use, depletion, and renewal of resources
- the nature of systems: social, cultural, political, and natural
- the structure of systems
- energy within systems: running down, exploding, and providing new energy to continue operation
- the relationship between parts and wholes; for example, between individuals and nations or between people and the natural environment

- the fit between a system or action and the environment it exists within, for example, the fit between strip mining and the human and natural communities in which it occurs, or the fit between the development of a particular community and its surroundings
- the study of changes over time, which is not necessarily the study of progress. This would look at how parts of the earth changed and affected each other over various time spans: over 10; 100; 1,000; 10,000; 100,000; and 1,000,000 years.
- the imaginative study of the future, the analysis of current trends, and the projection of future developments, as well as the imaginative construction of decent futures.

These subjects can be joined with action: recycling with the study of cycles; care of the local environment with the study of development. It is possible for five- and six-year-olds to run an entire recycling program with the help of a few adults and for high school students to participate in the development of community and regional general plans.

The habit of understanding cycles, wholes, and the part one's actions can play in creating a decent self-renewed life, as well as the habit of acting itself, can be developed and sustained throughout life in school. It can also help people come to a sense of the meaning and importance in their lives of what they can do as individuals and within groups. This feeling of empowerment, of each person's sense that he or she can be an effective part of the whole, is a basic contribution public education can make to the continuation and renewal of democratic ideas in our society.

The principles and ideas for renewal suggested here are:

1. Help students become lifelong learners.
2. End studies with suggestions for future learning and exploration.
3. Continued learning in groups should be encouraged through student-initiated and -taught classes.
4. Playing well should be a value in the curriculum and there

should be many different opportunities to experiment with play throughout school life.

5. Students should be given opportunities to teach and serve the school and community.

6. Classes on how to teach, ways of being of service without being condescending, how to tackle a problem with your friends, and so on, should be offered.

7. Ecological action should be accompanied by the study of systems, cycles, energy, and the renewal of resources.

These are all ways of preparing young people to apply the basic skills they learn in school throughout their lives.

A Basic-Skills Curriculum

A basic-skills curriculum adequate to the demands of democratic citizenship would include six major strands: language, thought, invention and discovery, expression, social understanding, and learning for oneself and service to others. These six skill areas can be organized in many different ways. The simplest but not necessarily the most productive way would be to have a six-subject day, providing an hour for each subject. It would also be possible to integrate these subjects about a theme and study the theme from different perspectives. For example, themes like:

- the development of computing devices from inscriptions on clay tablets to microcomputers
- utopian ideas of society
- the development of weaving and the design of fabrics

can be studied from the six different perspectives. Even such an unlikely theme as myths and monsters of the world can be integrative and studied

1. Linguistically, through poetry, transcriptions of oral recitations, and the creating and writing of new myths.

2. Intellectually, as symbolic ways of thinking and describing views of the world, or structurally, as ways of describing indirectly philosophical and social conflicts.
3. Artistically, through the representation of mythic beings and tales in painting, sculpture, theater, and cinema. The creation of new works or the reworking of old themes (such as the old Greek theater contests) could also be a part of this work.
4. Mechanically, through the myths of great inventors like Daedalus, Leonardo, Henry Ford, and Thomas Edison. This strand can also deal with the process of invention and the use of symbol and myth as conceptual devices that lead inventors on. The flying machine and horseless carriage had long mythical existences before they were transformed into physical realities.
5. Socially, through studying the use of myth to relate social structure and teach group values.
6. The study of myths of personal and group renewal and of the problems and rewards of service to others.

A school year could be organized around a half dozen themes, or two themes could be considered each year for a month at a time, the rest of the time being reserved for the simple six-class-a-day program.

There are bolder ways of organizing the basic skills, involving work in the community, the development of science and expression centers, the choosing of a central emphasis (such as expression or social life) and relating the other basics to that. Each school, each community, could develop a unique feasible way of organizing a basic education program that would fit with its resources, the specific needs and cultures of its students, and the nature of what is possible in the current political and economic situation.

In developing a program, it is essential to keep in mind the ultimate goals of teaching these basic skills. These are to provide young people with the skills required to deal with information, act effectively, and balance self-fulfillment with service, essential to positive participation in a democracy.

The ideas presented here might seem utopian, unobtainable in the immediate future. That is no reason to give up on them, just as the current antidemocratic climate is no reason to give up on democracy. Moreover, many of these ideas have been put into practice and others easily could. It is worth considering some examples of basic skills in action, and of examining how students can practice democracy in order to learn to be active, sensitive, and intelligent citizens.

Basic Skills in Action

Skills become internalized and mastered through being used. This simple observation is often overlooked in designing educational programs and is the basis for the common complaints of most students that they don't do anything in school. The key word in their complaint is "do." These students are not educational problems. They do well in their classes, they participate in athletics and other school activities. Yet they feel they don't do anything. What is the "do" that is missing? An analysis of school life answers the question quite clearly. Young people are required to learn math but don't use it; they write what they're assigned but see no use of writing other than to please the teacher or occasionally write a letter; they study history and geography and feel powerless to act in a messed-up world, and even when they study ecology and environmental issues, they can't mobilize themselves to clean up the trash in the schoolyard, much less participate in larger public actions. A good example of this occurred in my community recently. A controversy raged over whether or not oil should be drilled on- and offshore. In all the community meetings, commission hearings, and efforts to research the issue and document one's side, I do not recollect one young person (not even a high school student) who participated. The teachers at the school avoided the issue in class and a few even used "professionalism" as a way of avoiding taking personal stands. One community person did try to present the case against oil development but she was prevented from talking about oil by administration. Yet the lives of young people in our community will be profoundly affected by the choice between the development of oil and the development of alternate energy sources. They should know both sides, be encouraged to research and debate the issue, and, once having made up their minds, do something. They should be encouraged to act with the adults in the community, to participate in the social and political lives of their communities. They should be encouraged to practice democracy, not just in school but at all the forums of the community. This doesn't imply that the school should be for or against oil. What it does imply is that students should be engaged in gathering information about issues that will affect their lives, weighing that information, and taking reasoned positions on those issues. If students are to become effective citizens, they must learn to act effectively on a personal and group level. They must therefore get opportunities to practice the basic skills.

Action programs that give students an opportunity to exercise skills are an essential part of education. Here are some programs that could give students these opportunities.

Personal Action

There are many decisions that face young people and many more that will face them as adults. These decisions will affect their health, the quality of their lives, the work they do, and the ability they will have to maintain caring relationships with other people. The habit of passivity can be damaging and one has to wonder whether there isn't some natural transition from mechanically filling in ditto masters in schools to mechanically adopting social habits like smoking and drinking, to accepting TV watching and boring work as the nature of existence. I know some people who

162 · BASIC SKILLS

complain that life has seemed like one great big purple ditto master to them, that they never felt in control of their actions or able to act effectively on their decisions, and who woke up at forty to realize that they had hardly begun to live or know themselves.

School cannot solve all the problems of passivity and despair that exist in our society. But it can contribute something to avoiding them by assisting and encouraging students to "do" things. On a personal level this could mean showing students how to care for their own bodies: how to heal themselves as much as possible and how to develop and use their bodies effectively. This could consist of everything from teaching young people how to set broken bones, administer artificial respiration, and take and understand blood pressure readings, to developing health profiles for themselves and learning how to control stress and anxiety. The emphasis should be on prevention, on the development of a sensible understanding of how to keep your body well and your mind capable of dealing with stress.

Each school can have a small clinic staffed by a medical paraprofessional and students. The clinic would provide medical exams and advice on nonserious illness and on the care of the body and mind. Students would take responsibility for examining other students as well as themselves. A clear and responsible program would have to be developed to support such a clinic. Those functions that could only be performed by a doctor or medical technician would naturally not be done by youngsters. But it is likely that, with adequate supervision and training, children as young as seven or eight can do much that is now left in the hands of medical professionals. In these miniclinics students could do things for themselves and others: provide training in meditation, give information about vitamins and diet, monitor vital signs, and help each other with managing pain and stress.

An extension of the clinic could be made to the area of nutrition, though a better idea might be to have students take turns running the food-services operation with the help of adults, and integrate nutrition with eating, something rarely done in schools.

In either case, young people would be dealing with questions in the real world such as:

- How can Robert become less nervous?
- How do I deal with headaches?
- What is the best way to deal with pimples?
- How can I lose weight or stop eating so much?
- What does it cost to run a lunch program?
- How can lunches be cheap and taste good?
- What's the simplest way to clean up?

The crucial thing about classes involving personal action is that they are not studies of how other people act or how one could act. They involve direct action by students as well as planning. Here are a number of action units designed to enable young people to take control over their lives. They can be worked in as part of other aspects of a comprehensive program or can be separate classes that last for several weeks or a month at a time, which could be called times of "doing."

1. Building a small house. I've always dreamed of building a two-room cabin with six-, seven-, and eight-year-olds. We could begin by making a model and by looking at sheds and other small structures in the area. The students could use handtools and the teacher use power tools when they're called for. If you could build, wire, and plumb a small shed (and one could) by nine, imagine what you could learn to help you keep your home or apartment in repair after twelve years of school.
2. Strip down and rebuild motors, small generators, and metal machinery. Build a machine shop and make your own machine tools — and create your own tools.
3. Build and sail a boat.
4. Make all the furniture used at the school and use the money

previously used on furniture to support personal or group projects.

5. Train students to teach reading and turn the reading program for five-, six-, and seven-year-olds over to older children.

6. Set up a nursery and have students learn skills of nurturing young babies by doing it, as well as learning about it. This might provide a useful service to other members of the community as well as personal knowledge to young boys and girls. Teachers and other community members could bring their children.

7. Set up instruments to monitor environmental conditions and develop programs that can continue over the years to analyze weather, pollution, and meteorological trends.

Effective Action in Groups

Many people never learn to work with others toward a common goal. In school, with the exception of athletics, band, theater, and other extracurricular or minor subjects, every student is made into a loner. Moreover, group activities are almost entirely adult initiated and supervised. The consequence is that young people don't know how to initiate productive group activity (unless they learn how at home or on the streets), and that they internalize the attitude that they cannot be trusted to function in groups. This is one of the main attitudes that has to be combated if there is to be any hope that they will come together and solve common social, economic, and cultural problems as adults. Young people should be given opportunities to plan and execute activities without overriding adult supervision and should not look upon mutual assistance as perverse and damaging to one's standing in the competitive school hierarchy.

Young people should be accustomed to being part of self-initiated and self-regulating groups, and teachers should learn how to become resources at times, and not feel a need to control, direct, or supervise some student activities. There are a number of ways to achieve these goals and to enable young people to relate to the world beyond school while still in school. One particularly interesting attempt to assist youngsters to act effectively in groups was tried at the St. Paul Open School, a kindergarten-through-twelfth-grade alternative school within the St. Paul public school system. Through the Consumer Action Service, a project of the Protect Your Rights and Money class that Joe Nathan taught at the school, students took on a collective community battle that affected their lives. Karen Branan and Joe Nathan described the project in an article published in *Learning:*

> The whole thing started six years ago when a group of St. Paul Open School students, who were studying ecology with Nathan, began to notice "a stinky stench" in their heavily industrialized school neighborhood. They traced the smells to four sources: a paper plant and three food processing and packing plants. An investigation and action project ensued.
>
> Students talked with people at the Minnesota Public Interest Research Group. Spent hours at the Environmental Library studying odor pollution standards for every state. Consulted lawyers. Called for plant inspection by the city's Pollution Control Agency. Worked with the agency to write official complaints. Petitioned residents and other businesses affected by the odors. Testified at a public PCA hearing. Got the runaround from company and public officials. Persisted, persisted, persisted.
>
> And won.
>
> The PCA found the plants in violation of pollution ordinances and ordered schedules of compliance from each of the plants.
>
> This project planted the seeds of the Consumer Action Service. Nathan believed that the youthful idealism, enthusiasm and intensity displayed in the pollution project could be directed toward solving a variety of relatively small problems that Twin City consumers encountered. At the same time, students would develop important skills in such diverse areas as writing business letters, using telephones and telephone directories, dealing with government and business organizations, and knowing their own rights and responsibilities.

Thriving in its second year, Consumer Action Service (CAS) deals in diversity: Dobermans and rental deposits, automobiles and insurance, shampooers and busted water pipes. The group (30 children currently are in the class) has worked on more than fifty cases and boasts a successful resolution rate of over 75 per cent.[40]

There is no reason why students cannot be actively involved in the functioning of government as well as in consumer issues. It is essential for citizens of a democracy not to be afraid of, or awed by, the people they elect to represent them. Students should get to know the people who run government even if it causes slight inconveniences. This means more than a single court visit or a tour of the state capital. It means looking at committees and task forces, departments and subdepartments, at public works, highway and building departments. There are enough branches of government that affect our lives to provide young people with more experience than they would probably want or need. The exercise of power through government can be learned through apprenticeships; through studying a single voting district; through following a bill, initiated by one's local representative, through the legislature; by following a building inspector or county supervisor about for a time as if one were a national journalist in a Presidential candidate's party; and by working for candidates one supports on their election campaigns. The constant presence of young people may be annoying to people who exercise political power, but it might have the bonus of keeping their constituencies in mind more than some politicians are accustomed to doing. We should and can devise ways that make it possible for students to experience how people work at politics on an everyday basis.

In addition, young people should have experience exercising power. Every school ought to have student governance over areas of life that don't need adult control. This can range all the way from the management of discipline problems to planning a school dance or to setting up the athletic schedule for the year. Students can run and edit a newspaper, and, given modern minitechnology, control their own radio and video stations. As a general principle, one shouldn't do things for students, or control them, if there is a way to assist them in doing it themselves.

It is even possible for young people to become engaged in sensible political activities on a worldwide scale. I am currently working with Cynthia Brown and Eileen Malloy of Amnesty International on a project that would make it possible for young people to act together to assist prisoners of conscience throughout the world. Amnesty, an international organization based in London, won the Nobel Prize for Peace in 1977. The London office of Amnesty investigates reports of individual or group violations of human rights. The organization adopts prisoners throughout the world that have been documented to have been jailed (or in the case of Argentina, for example, "disappeared"; or in Russia, committed to mental institutions) for their beliefs and who have not been involved in acts of violence. Amnesty itself has no political orientation. It currently has adopted prisoners from Russia, the United States, and throughout most of the world. In order to avoid accusations of meddling with the internal affairs of a government, Amnesty also has adopted the policy that an Amnesty group in one country must work for the release of prisoners in other countries. Thus the Amnesty groups in the United States adopt prisoners from everywhere with the exception of the United States, and write letters, make phone calls, and on occasion make prison visits and monitor trials in order to release the adopted prisoners they are assigned by the London office.

Amnesty also runs an Emergency Action Network which deals with helping people in immediate danger of death or torture, or with people who have disappeared. It responds immediately to crisis situations and sends out daily letters to different groups and individuals who have volunteered to help.

It occurred to me that some students might want to give

time to helping prisoners throughout the world and at the same time discover the social, political, and economic conditions in other places. I contacted Scott and Ellen Harrison of the San Francisco office of Amnesty and Cynthia Brown, who works with me at the Coastal Ridge Research and Education Center, and they were enthusiastic about doing an Amnesty curriculum and involving young people in the work of Amnesty. We joined together and produced a curriculum called Conscience and Human Rights. The curriculum was tested in 250 schools and is available through Amnesty.

It provides materials for the study of *acts of conscience* and shows how young people can become involved in the Emergency Action Network or in an Amnesty Action Group. It gives young people an opportunity to be effective in the world and, through membership in adoption groups, enables them to participate as peers with adults of all ages in important social and moral activity.

Not all forms of effective group action need be this serious. Young people should have experience organizing dances and games, in running tournaments, and should have a voice in deciding upon the allocation of school resources. In small schools it is possible to have a town forum in which students and teachers bring up issues of local concern and decide upon common action. In larger schools some form of elected representative body could do the same thing.

Most student governments in our schools have no real power. Teachers cannot be questioned, community issues are avoided, bad teaching habits cannot be mentioned, subjects that interest students and are not being taught cannot be initiated, school discipline is not dealt with. The faculty advisor monitors the agenda and usually confines it to harmless issues like dances, support for athletics, and the purchase of uniforms for the cheerleaders. The council also usually has no power to act without the approval of the faculty advisor and administrators.

However, it is possible to establish student councils and town forums that have power to deal with certain educational, financial, personnel, and social issues. This doesn't mean that students should control all aspects of the school's programs. They shouldn't, since they are only passing through, while the teachers provide continuity and, presumably, know things students don't yet know and, therefore, can't control sensibly. Areas can be carved out, however, where students (or students and teachers together) have power. These can relate to teacher evaluation, the development of new programs, the allocation of funds in certain areas of the budget, the development of discipline policies in the schools, and so on.

I expect people to object that students are likely to make mistakes if they are given power. The only reply I can make is that making mistakes is part of making choices, and that if one is worried about mistakes, simply look at the state of public education now. We have to let students make small mistakes in order to correct large mistakes in current practice.

There is another form of group action that comes to mind. It could be called mutual study. There is an African saying that a group moves at the speed of its slowest member. This saying is used in the context of arguing for mutual assistance. Students can help each other to learn, can share knowledge, can take a responsibility for the performance of the group they belong to as well as for their own performance. That's hard to do within a grading system that only rewards individual functioning. Group values have to be reintegrated into the moral life of young people at school. We have to be ingenious and persistent in trying to convince each of our students of the value of all of them, and create ways of rewarding mutual assistance as well as individual achievement.

There are two other areas where schools can help young people act effectively and exercise basic skills. They are in the world of work and in learning to use the resources of the earth sensibly. In the world of work it is important for young people to have experience:

- finding out what kind of work there is to do
- knowing how to seek employment
- working in different forms of business, some based on a management/labor model, others on worker control or cooperative models
- have experience with unions and other worker organizations and learn what it is to organize to protect the interests of working people
- knowing what it costs to live simply without hunger or major discomfort and relate that to the actual income of different forms of work
- learning how to increase one's power by pooling resources with others
- perhaps most importantly, having experience working at different jobs and learning what is right for you; what gives you pleasure, as well as money, so that you can strive to do nurturing work instead of being drained forty hours a week.

There are a number of ways these ideas can be realized. Schools can set up small businesses that are student run and serve modest community needs. A print- or bakeshop, a small furniture- or toy-making business can fit in well with most any educational program. These businesses can be organized in different ways, though given my own political and economic preferences, I believe in student cooperatives based on collective controls, which could be small models of economic and social democracy in action.

In addition to these businesses, students can go into the community and work as apprentices. It might even be in the interest of the unions and the corporations to open themselves up to young people and identify good workers.

The last form of effective action I want to mention is that of learning how to use the resources of the earth sensibly. Schools should provide the opportunities for students to:

Learn how to grow food and raise gardens. We need urban gardens, small poultry operations, even farms in the city if necessary. At the same time, young people ought to learn about the effects of herbicides and preservatives, to experiment with different forms of food production, to experience growing cycles, and experience how much a well-tended small plot (even on the fire escape of an apartment) can produce. It is important to learn how things grow and not be stuck at the end of the food production cycle, eating whatever comes in the prettiest box. These activities can, for example, be integrated into classes on technology, science, and tools.

The idea of a gardening project that integrates agriculture with ecology, science, and economics is, of course, not new. Recently I encountered a description of one such project that was carried out at the Norris School in the early 1930s. The Norris School was set up for newly settled TVA workers and the gardening project became the Norris School Cooperative:

> The general science teacher and pupils in his junior high school classes conceived the idea of planning their work around certain community needs. The class made arrangements with the town management to rent four acres of ground. The stated purpose of the group was to garden. Fresh vegetables were in demand and the children were anxious to earn some money. The teacher's purpose was that, and more. He wanted to guide his class in a meaningful study of soil chemistry, seed germination, erosion, cultivation, selection, bacteriology, etc.
>
> The problem of raising necessary finances and of organizing the work confronted them. The group then called to its assistance the social studies teacher. He led them into the study of the various forms of business organization, and after careful consideration they decided that the co-operative form of organization was best suited to their purposes. The problem of raising money to purchase seed, equipment, and fertilizer and to pay the rent was involved. The mathematics teacher, seeing an opportunity, adjusted her program to in-

clude consideration of the vital needs of this group and as-
sisted them by teaching them to compute interest and percentage, to make graphs, to figure fractions, and to weigh and
measure. The English teacher helped the group by assisting
them to talk effectively, to write letters, and to prepare advertising copy. Soon there were four teachers from different
subject fields working together with children on a project
that very naturally overlapped and cut across subject matter
fields. This co-operative has grown and continues to be a
most interesting development. The activities now include
gardening, a school bank, the school cafeteria, and other en-
terprises. It is conducted according to accepted principles
and practices for production co-operatives. Pupils of the
three junior high school years may belong and usually the
entire group elects to join. This project has existed for four
years. In some respects the work of the co-operative is the
"core" activity for the junior high school years. Those pupils
who develop or discover special interests enroll in subject
matter courses of their choice. Thus the activity program
and the course offerings merge to form the curriculum for
the child.[41]

*Learn about how different forms of energy can be trans-
lated into work, and explore solar, wind, coal, petroleum,
manual, and other forms of energy by running experimental
energy plants at the school and by participating in local
energy politics.*

*Develop a planning shop in each school that would be
devoted to studying and acting upon zoning and planning
issues.* These could range from population density to the
placement of industry and residences; to the effects of oil
spills on animal life, to the development of a community
beautification program and the painting of community mu-
rals. The first reference I've seen to this idea was in a booklet
entitled *You and Your Community: A Primer,* written by
the prominent architects Oscar Stonorov and Louis Kahn in
1944.[42] In the pamphlet, which attempts to introduce people

to the importance of their personal participation in the process of community planning, the authors propose that each school set up a shop where students build models of their community and develop alternate plans for neighborhood revitalization or development.

I would go further and extend the activities of the planning shop, especially for older children, to the shops of professional planners and developers. There is also no reason why students couldn't take an active part in controversies over the nature of community preservation and development, as well as present their plans for serious consideration by public officials.

It's interesting that Stonorov and Kahn begin their pamphlet with this quote from Lewis Mumford's "Faith for Living," which sets the planning shop in a larger ecological context:

> The final test of an economic system is not the tons of iron, the tanks of oil, or the miles of textiles it produces: the final test lies in its ultimate products — the sorts of men and women it nurtures and the order and beauty and sanity of their communities.[43]

All of these forms of basic skills in action have common goals: illustrating through practice that young people can have the power to control major parts of their lives, and that acting with, rather than against, others can provide a nurturing existence for all of us. They involve the exercise of thought and imagination; the intelligent use of language; a sensitive understanding of people in groups; and the use of science, technology, and tools in the service of people. They give basic skills human substance.

One question that comes to many people's minds in examining these ideas is Where do reading, writing, and arithmetic fit in? The answer is, almost everywhere. They are indispensable tools. But what, you could ask, of the skills themselves, the times tables, the alphabet, punctuation and grammar? Where do children encounter those? I would say that children should encounter those through their application, that letters and words should be encountered through books and signs and papers and magazines; that times tables should be encountered through what my son calls timesing, through understanding that it is easier to calculate the sum of fifteen dimes by multiplying 15×10 than by adding $10+10+10+10+10+10+10+10+10+10+10+10+10+10$ $+10$; that grammar and punctuation can be encountered through the study of language history and linguistics. Many students will learn to read, punctuate, and multiply without the need for any drill. Some can benefit from drill, from a deck of flash cards, a focused phonics lesson, or a brief lesson on punctuation. If the content is meaningful and interesting there will be a reason for students to discipline themselves and undergo a bit of drill. However, there is no point in drill for the sake of control or as a substitute for content. Drill, phonics, or other mechanical learning should only be provided when they are needed in specific instances, and should assume their proper modest place in a rich basic-skills curriculum.

PART FIVE

What Can We Do Now?

It IS OBVIOUSLY EASIER to dream of an ideal public education than to make it happen. Nothing can change all at once or begin to function smoothly without years of mistakes and experimentation. Moreover, there is no single formula for change that will work in every public school in the United States. Thinking of the public schools reminds me of the first line of Leo Tolstoy's *Anna Karenina:* "All happy families resemble one another, but each unhappy family is unhappy in its own way." No matter how much one can generalize the problems of public education, each school that is not serving its students has its unique weaknesses and problems. The tensions within the school, the relation of the teachers to the community, the internal staff struggles, the history of education within the community, the economic conditions of the parents as well as their culture, all give each school a character that has to be analyzed and dealt with if change is to occur. This means that it is essential to find ways of studying the present conditions of schools, pinpointing the places where change is most likely to occur, drawing up a list of priorities for new programs and structures, and then proceeding to organize and act. In some communities change can be initiated through the development of an arts or science program. In others it might come from an attack on standardized testing, or the development of cultural and human studies. It's possible that one community can mobilize enough support and capital to develop a center for science and the arts while another can get support for a large-scale community apprenticeship program. One has to begin somewhere, acknowledging the larger goals, and remembering that it will be a long struggle but one that is central to the survival of democracy in our society.

In order to undertake the often unrewarding task of revitalizing and reconstructing public education, one has to have clarity about the nature and effectiveness of one's own education. It is important before jumping into educational conflict to take time to think about your own educational history, and those of your friends and relatives. Perhaps then an analysis of the present and projections for the future can be grounded in a fuller, more informed sense of the complexities of the past. To facilitate such questioning and recollection, here is a *Good-Old-Days Basic-Skills Questionnaire* that you might like to fill out and share with other people you know who are interested in defining and solving some of the problems of public education.

Good-Old-Days Basic-Skills Questionnaire

1. *Try to recollect your years in school: call up faces, tones, the ambiance of the classrooms you lived in, your own feelings as a child in school.*
   a. Which teachers did you like? Why? Are there any common characteristics you noticed? What did you do as a way of expressing your affection? How did being with them affect what you learned?
   b. Which teachers did you dislike? Why specifically did you dislike them? Are there common characteristics? If not, what are the different reasons you didn't like them? What did you do as a way of expressing your hostility? How did being in their class affect your learning?
   c. Are there any teachers whom you didn't like but whom you respected? Why was that combination possible? How did being with them affect what you learned?
   d. Were there any teachers you liked who you think didn't teach you anything worth learning? Why did you like them?

2. *Remember your report cards.*
   a. Do you think you were graded fairly?
   b. Do you think the grades helped you learn or made it harder to learn?
   c. How did you feel handing your report card to your parents?
   d. How did your parents respond to your grades and how did their responses affect your learning and behavior in school?

3. *What do you feel that you learned in school that has been of value in your life? Try to be as specific as possible. Think of*
   a. everyday practical living
   b. personal relationships
   c. work life
   d. things you do for pleasure
   e. your participation in social activities
   f. your participation in political life
   g. your current economic situation.

4. *Did anything that happened during your time in school substantially change the way you look at and participate in activities in the world?*
   a. Do you feel you were empowered by school?
   b. What do you do that you wouldn't otherwise do because of your school experience?

5. *What roles do the three Rs play in your life?*
   a. How do you use reading, writing, and arithmetic in your life?
   b. Have you acquired or developed any of those skills since leaving school or outside of school?
   c. Do you feel confident using those skills?
   d. Do you think from the perspective of an adult that you were taught these skills in ways that increased your power and enriched your life?
   e. Were the skills you need to function acquired in school? How and when? If not, where and how did you acquire them?

6. *Would you like your children to attend exactly the same school you did as a child?*
   a. If so, why? Does it have to do with how good your school seemed or how bad theirs is?
   b. If not, why? Is it because of how good theirs seems or how bad yours was? What would not be good for your children to be exposed to?

7. *Did you ever question things in school or in any way protest what was happening to you?*
   a. Was the protest private, within your mind, or expressed to a small number of friends?
   b. Did you ever act on your own or with others to express criticism at school?
   c. Did you ever wish you did more than you could to express your feelings and opinions?
   d. Did you ever defy school indirectly — by damaging a book, breaking a window, writing graffiti? Did your friends? Did you ever wish you did?

8. *Were there any times when your parents would defend you against school authorities?*
   a. Did you ever get in trouble?
   b. Did you ever get in trouble righteously — that is, when you believed you were right and the school authorities were wrong?
   c. Did any adults defend you?
   d. Were your parents afraid of school authorities? What was their attitude to school? How did that affect what you learned and how you behaved?

9. *Did your parents ever talk to you about their own schooling?*
   a. How did their educational experiences affect the way they treated you as a student?
   b. Did they have, in your opinion, an accurate sense of what went on in your classes and realistic expectations for school learning?

10. *Try to reconstruct a day you spent in elementary school, junior high school, and high school. Begin waking up in the*

morning and end finishing homework and putting school out of your mind for a while. Did you ever put school out of your mind those days?

11. *As a final exercise, compare your school with those your children attend. Has much changed? What specifically are the pluses and minuses of both situations? If you have the time, go through this questionnaire with your children. Compare the answers they give with those you gave, and with those you expected they would give.*

Your Child's School Questionnaire

The information provided by thinking through or writing out answers to the questionnaire on your own educational history will obviously not provide an objective analysis of the state of public education in the past and present. However, it can get you to thinking about schools and to asking intelligent questions about the effectiveness of current practice. The next steps are to visit your local school, attend school-board meetings, and gather information that can help you develop a strategy for change.

Here are a few outlines that can assist you in interpreting classroom and school observation, interviewing teachers, and finding out how money is being spent in your local school district.

Educational Profile

There are a number of things you can learn through informal observations that can be useful later on if resistance to change develops. Here are some things you might look for:

1. Where are the students most miserable or bored? Look at their faces, at the way they respond in class. And ask them on the playground what they think about the school. Ask several times, not just once, as young people are often

cautious and noncommittal when they respond to people they don't know.

2. Try to find out where the students feel most comfortable as well as which adults they like and respect. Often these people can become your allies. Change can most effectively happen when parents and teachers work together.

3. What role does testing play in the school's program? Does it assist or inhibit learning? How?

4. What opportunities do students have to use in personally rewarding and constructive ways the skills being taught?

Classroom Observation

Classroom observation takes a bit of skill and experience. The goal of the observer is to melt into the wall, to have the students and teachers forget you are there. For that reason, it is important to stay for at least an hour, to return at least once, and to be quiet and unobtrusive. It is impossible for a teacher and students to present a show for long, and if you are patient, you will be able to observe their natural life together and see how they function without observers.

Here's a list of specific things to watch for in a classroom that might help organize your observations:

1. What do the walls say? Is there evidence of student work? Is the work recent? Is it the "best" work of a few students, or does it represent efforts of most of the students? Is there nothing on the walls at all? Or are there teacher-made or bought displays with no apparent student input?

2. Building on this, is there any evidence of process in the room? Are there things in different stages of development about the room or is everything finished? Are there working spaces and storage spaces where work in progress can be done and protected?

3. How much nonpaperwork is done in the class? Is science done on mimeo sheets or with scientific apparatus? Is there any evidence of the arts being used in other areas of curriculum such as social studies, science, reading, math?

4. Observing the interactions of teachers and students, is there any evidence of teaching? That is, does the teacher assign pages in a text and correct papers or are there lectures, demonstrations, individual explanations, experiments?

5. How much time is spent on textbook and workbook activity and how much for other forms of functioning? What evidence is there of nontextbook learning?

6. What evidence can you find of learning? Observe the students during a lesson. How do their faces look? How many are paying attention? Do you find excitement, interest, thought, boredom, anger? What is the learning tone of the situation: interest, resistance, or indifference?

7. Who talks? How much? What is their mode of speech? Who asks questions? Are the questions open or close-ended? Do students question? Does the teacher give thoughtful answers? Is there evidence of dialogue, of students and teacher being interested in each other and what they're learning?

8. Is there evidence of sharing in the class? Of competition? Which is sanctioned? What are the rewards and punishments that characterize the social situation?

9. Is there evidence of favoritism or discrimination? This could range from seating arrangements to special grouping, to teacher's tone of voice, or selectivity in calling on students, criticizing them, or praising them.

10. Is there any sign that students enjoy being in the class? Evidence of thought or problem solving?

11. What content is being dealt with in the class? Does the content match student interest in any way?

12. Does the teacher give the impression of wanting to be with the children or would he or she rather be somewhere else?

13. Who makes the decisions? Is there any evidence of student decision making?

14. Does humiliation play any role in this classroom? Are bad examples used to humiliate violators and good ones to shame them?

15. Do you think the students want to be in that classroom with that teacher? Would you as a young person enjoy being there, or at least feel it would benefit you?

These are only a few things you can look for. You'll see a lot more by observing a few times and it makes sense to take notes on what you see that is positive or negative. A last and major thing to look for is evidence of students learning to function in democratic ways. Do students have any power and any responsibility? Do they have group discussions and make group decisions? Do they care about their environment and have a say in determining how it is used and structured? Is there evidence of the intelligent use of language, of thought and the exercise of the imagination, of learning to use tools and technology and of the exercise of human sensitivity at the school? In other words, are the basic skills being taught?

Teacher Conference
It is also important to go directly to the teachers to get information about their goals and practice. It is also valuable for teachers to try to articulate their philosophy of learning and examine how it affects their classroom practice.

Teachers often do not have articulated goals and so sometimes you have to ask specific questions and develop a conversation in which goals (or lack of them) are articulated informally. Here's a list of questions that can help teachers articulate their goals. (Though the questions are framed from the parents' point of view, they can be used by teachers who want to examine their own practice and are committed to improving public education.)

1. What are the most important things you'd like to see your students learn?
2. Do all of your students manage to learn them?
3. What things do you do when you find a student just isn't learning?
4. How do you teach reading?
5. What do you think it is important for your students to read?
6. What do you think will become of your students in the future?

7. What do you like to teach best?
8. Are there any things you'd like to teach that you don't have time to get to?
9. Do you have an educational philosophy or do you work on a practical basis doing what you feel is best at a particular time?
10. If you have a philosophy what is it? If not, what guides your practice?
11. How do you deal with discipline problems? break up fights? deal with unhappy children?
12. What is the balance between cooperation and competition you would like to see in your classroom?
13. Are there any specific children or kinds of children you feel you're particularly good with? are there any you just can't reach?
14. Do cultural differences play any role in how you teach? do intellectual differences? class differences?
15. Have you ever visited what you would call an ideal school or classroom? Describe it. How has experiencing it affected your work?

The information that you get from this informal profile will be of great help in drawing up a list of priorities for the change of your school.

A Cost-of-Education Profile

In addition to learning what goes on in the classroom, there is another form of information that will also be indispensable: that is information on how much it costs to educate a child currently and what the cost of changing things might be. This means specifically how much is spent in direct services to children and how much is siphoned off for administration, district overhead, and other non-child-related functions.

A major reason to examine the budget beginning with direct services to children is that if cuts have to be made in school budgets, or if changes are to be made in programs, we have to be sure that the children are not the ones who suffer while the hierarchies are protected. The effects of tax limitation initiatives, such as Proposition 13 in California, are perfect examples of how not to make school cuts. The first programs to go were at the bottom: instructional aides, music, art, library programs. The hierarchies stayed intact. Because of the hierarchial nature of public school systems, it was the people up in the hierarchy who made the decision about what was to go. Everyone cut someone lower down, when, from the point of view of preserving the quality of education in a fiscally depressed situation, the cuts should have been made in the middle and at the top. In many cases, we have money to make substantial positive changes in public education if we could cut, or eliminate, the fat middle, the bloated nonteaching staff of most school districts.

Financial information is sometimes very hard to get because money is often shifted around school bureaucracies to hide the simple fact that too little is spent directly on the education of children.

The first time I saw a school district purchasing catalog I was astonished. The prices the district was paying for supplies like chalk and paper, and for books, was higher than some items cost retail and higher than all of them cost at bargain outlets. In addition, I noticed that the district had several high-paid purchasing agents, a number of secretaries, a fully staffed warehouse, as well as several trucks and drivers all employed in the ordering and distribution of supplies and books. In addition, I discovered that the district had no inventory of what was in the warehouse and what was in the schools. The explanation given for a lack of inventory was that things moved too fast from the warehouse to the schools, and that there were too many consumables to make it possible to keep an accurate inventory. Knowing from my teaching experience that the opposite was true, that things hardly moved at all from warehouse to classroom, and that it was common to receive books and supplies one or two years late (if you got them at all), I decided to pursue the issue. It occurred to me that supplies and books could be purchased more efficiently and inexpensively on an individual school or classroom basis, and I asked the director of purchasing what the advantages of centralized purchasing were. He informed me that it led to increased efficiency and savings. I asked what figures he used to draw those conclusions and the response was, it was his job to run the purchasing operation. The financial department would provide the figures.

I went to the financial division of the district. It was staffed by an administrator of assistant-superintendent status, two teachers, an accountant, a bookkeeper, two computer programmers, and several secretaries. The financial office also had its own building, its own custodian, its expense and supply budget. However, it had no information on how it was determined that centralized purchasing was more efficient (or cost effective, as it is called in the jargon) than decentralized individual school purchasing. In fact, I couldn't even get a school-by-school breakdown of supplies ordered and money spent, nor a budget that showed all the costs of running a centralized food-services operation, and use those to determine whether it wouldn't be cheaper (and more educationally effective and nutritional) to run on-site food and nutrition programs.

My frustration in digging information out of a school bureaucracy is not exceptional. In Berkeley, for example, the Citizens Master Plan Facilities Committee issued a final report on June 15, 1978, whose first recommendation was that the school district "design and implement a procedure to generate and maintain site-specific information on costs, personnel, program capacities, and enrollment." In commenting on this recommendation, the committee said:

> The district can neither plan nor control its operations without an adequate data base. This committee's investiga-

tions have demonstrated numerous shortcomings in both the availability of data and its use by the district. The absence of site-specific data has made it impossible for us to differentiate between sites on the basis of operating costs. More money might be saved through efficient management than through site closings, but no one will ever know unless the district substantially improves its capability to manage its affairs. Missing data on site-related costs is only one symptom of the larger problem — a general lack of capability to plan.[44]

The inability to relate expenditures to educational programs, and to evaluate how effective these expenditures are, is not a new problem for public education. For example, in 1916, the Cleveland Foundation did a survey of public education in that city and concluded that

> What is beginning to happen in Cleveland is what always happens when the business department of a Board of Education is made entirely independent of the educational department and the two are presided over by independent executives of equal rank. In such cases the danger is always that the business department will eventually come to regard its work as an end in itself and forget that the sole purpose for which it exists is to help in the great task of teaching thousands of children.[45]
> — Cleveland Education Survey, 1916

Seeing the inefficiency (deliberate or not) and remoteness from educational concerns of most finance departments, one can wonder whether the department itself couldn't be eliminated and each school given its own budget and held accountable for it. With the development of microcomputers, it is possible, for less than most school districts spend on renting large computers, to purchase a microcomputer and printer for each school, to train school secretaries and administrators in basic bookkeeping, accounting, and computer use, and have detailed school-by-school budgets printed out at the end of each month or quarter.

Getting sensible, well-organized financial information out of public education bureaucracies is almost impossible. Yet without such information it is difficult to answer questions such as:

- How much is being spent on direct services to children and how much on administration?
- How much does it cost to run an individual classroom in school?
- How much is spent on educational material that is used in the classroom (as opposed, say, to media equipment bought for administrative use)?
- What services can be done without?
- What services are inadequately performed because they are underfinanced?
- What would it cost to totally reorganize a public education system?

I believe that there should be no secrets about how public education money is spent, and educators should be held accountable for what they conceal. The crucial information that is needed is the current cost of running a school or classroom so that we can begin to estimate what it might cost to run an educational program based on some of the principles enumerated above. Economic information should be gathered from the bottom up, from the classroom to the school, dollar by dollar up the hierarchy, so that we can get a picture of the flow of money through a school system. School systems are not identical, so what is needed is a profile that will account for the uniqueness of each district and will give hints about how reconstruction can take place in specific places. It would be a mistake to believe that a single plan for rebuilding public education could be constructed and then applied automatically in every place. What we need are overall goals and specific information so that the goals can be translated into intelligent practice determined by the uniqueness of each situation.

FINANCIAL INFORMATION PROFILE

1. Average per pupil
   expenditure in dis-
   trict _____
   (This figure usually includes all money spent except for trans-
   portation and capital outlay.)

	Class	**School**
2. Number of pupils	_____	_____
3. Number of pupils x average per-pupil expenditure	_____	_____

(This figure is what would be spent if all money was spent in
classroom services or on a site level with no administration or
district-wide services.)

4. How money is actu-
   ally spent at school
   site
   A. *Salaries*

1. teacher(s)	_____	_____
2. aides	_____	_____
3. artists, scientists, community resources	_____	_____
4. custodial	_____	_____
5. food service workers	_____	_____

(For food service and custodial workers one can project
a per-classroom percentage of their salary, as they usually serve the whole school.)

B. *Supplies and books*

(This is the money spent on the supplies, not the services of the purchasing bureaucracies.)

	Class	School
1. textbooks	_____	_____
2. workbooks	_____	_____
3. library and general reading books	_____	_____
4. art supplies	_____	_____
5. science supplies	_____	_____
6. math supplies	_____	_____
7. paper, pencils, etc.	_____	_____
8. maintenance supplies	_____	_____
9. food-service supplies	_____	_____
10. other (specify)	_____	_____

C. *Administrators and education costs on school site*

1. administrators' salary	_____	_____
2. secretary, other administrative backups	_____	_____
3. administrative supplies, equipment budget	_____	_____

4. discretion-
   ary fund _____ _____
   (Most administrators are given a discretionary budget,
   which they can use for emergencies or for special school
   programs. This is used sometimes to reward teachers
   who are favored or to support programs there is community pressure for.)

5. testing _____ _____
   (Many school districts spend money to have standardized tests computer scored and have the results tabu-
   lated. It is usually not cheap to have this done and it is
   questionable whether this is necessary.)

6. consultants _____ _____
   (These are consultants hired by the teachers or administrators, not those chosen by the central bureaucracy
   and sent down to the school.)

D. *Special pro-
   grams budgets* _____ _____
   (Many schools have special programs for reading, handicapped children, or gifted children. These programs
   usually serve a small number of pupils. Some are important; some, such as programs for so-called educationally handicapped children, have questionable educational value. The programs and their budgets should
   be considered separately, though often they are lumped
   together.)

Program I	Number of students	Class	School
1. salaries	_____	_____	_____
2. supplies/books	_____	_____	_____
3. share of custodial services	_____	_____	_____
4. share food services	_____	_____	_____
5. other (e.g. physical therapy)	_____	_____	_____

Program II, etc.

E. *Teaching personnel: At school site without classroom assignment*
(These teachers are the specialists in math, reading, science, et cetera, who "wander," especially in schools where teachers have an hour of "release" time during the teaching day. The cost and effectiveness of these teachers should be considered carefully.)
Specialist I
1. salary   ——————————

2. supplies budget   ——————————

3. custodial share   ——————————

Here's an example of a class-cost profile in a school containing ten classrooms with average class size of thirty and average per-pupil expenditures of $2,000 per year.

1. Per pupil expenditure $ 2,000
2. Number pupils   30
3. Item 1 x Item 2 $60,000
4. Money spent in classroom
  A. *Salaries*
    1. Teacher salary $20,000
    2. Aides, ½ time $ 5,000
    3. Other people resources   0
    4. Custodial (1/10 of $10,000) $ 1,000
    5. Food service (1/10 of $5,000) $ 500
  B. *Supplies and Books*
    1. textbooks ($2.00 per pupil per year, four times the California state allotment of fifty cents) $ 60
    2. workbooks $ 60
    3. library/reading books $ 50
    4. art supplies $ 100
    5. science supplies $ 25
    6. math supplies $ 20
    7. paper, pencils, etc. $ 100

8. maintenance supplies   ✲
9. food service supplies   ✲
10. other   —

TOTAL SPENT DIRECTLY IN CLASSROOM $26,915

✲ These are hard figures to get. The other figures should be calculated by what actually arrives in a classroom, not what is ordered.

Thus the direct costs in this case are $26,915 compared to a total per-pupil income of $60,000. The difference of $33,085 must be examined carefully. There are certainly many school-wide services that are important and some district-wide services that are necessary to maintain quality and equality (such as people whose job is to implement a de-segregation program). However, each expense should be clearly listed.

The next step in examining the economics of education takes us out of the school classroom to the administration and then to the centralized bureaucracy. Here things get even murkier. The best thing to do is to get an organization chart of your school district plus a copy of the last few years' budgets and you might be able to tease out some useful information. It still makes sense to go from the bottom up, questioning every level of the school hierarchy in terms of how it serves the classroom and the individual school. Here's a simplified version of what you might find in a district of ten schools:

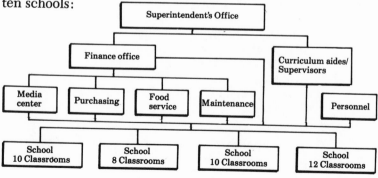

There are three levels in the hierarchy that exist to serve the school. The budgets of these hierarchies have to be uncovered, for it is usually very difficult to get information about them. One rough way is to estimate how much is actually being spent at the school sites for the services they purport to supply (for example, food service, maintenance, supplies) and subtract from the total budget. It will often get murkier the higher one gets, and my feeling is that if people won't provide figures you have some reason to presume that there might be some padding in the budget or at least some concern that unnecessary work is being created that does not serve the children.

The information provided by this questionnaire, as difficult as it might be to acquire, will not by itself tell us how to improve public education. It can help us pinpoint those aspects of current practice that should be eliminated or modified, but we also have to be bold enough to think of administrator-free school districts, decentralized financial structures, schools that are not organized on the basis of classrooms, and teachers who are qualified by what they know and have done, rather than by the teachers college they attended. This reexamination of public education should not be confused with budget slashing and economizing. It is foolish to economize when it comes to the lives of our children. We don't spend enough money for proper education for all the children in our society and should be committed to spending more. The problem I'm pointing out here is that, *even though we are not spending enough on schools, what we are spending is not being spent well.*

Thinking through one's own educational history and gathering information are preliminary steps to initiating the process of change. The next, more difficult, steps consist of listing your priorities for change at your own school, organizing people to work with you, and taking the first concrete actions that might lead to change.

It is sensible to initiate positive changes and initiate new programs while trying to eliminate negative practices. In my experience, attacks on public education that are not backed by a positive program for reconstruction fail even if they appear to succeed. They lead to bogus reform and accommodation, but not to fundamental change. One way to begin to conceive of positive change is to take a look at the strengths of your children and your community and begin to build from there.

Considering Your Strengths

School is only one of the many worlds young people are part of. When a child arrives at school at the age of four or five, he or she has family experiences, and is a member of one or several cultural and social groups as well as part of a culture of play involving other children. He or she also has most likely been exposed to TV, has traveled, seen cars and airplanes, messed around with paint, clay, and crayons, engaged in fantasy play with dolls (whether of the Barbie or Star Wars variety), and been exposed to the printed word through TV ads, billboards, packages, and books and newspapers. Four- and five-year-olds also (with very rare exceptions) have mastered a language, know something of music and dance, and make guesses about what the stars are really made of and how machines work. All the different modes of acquiring information, thinking, and imagining, are active before children ever reach school. Moreover, all these modes continue to be active outside of the school context throughout a student's school career. This is often forgotten by school people who treat students as if the only thing they could possibly know (other than what they brought to school with them at five) has been learned at school.

Any education program that will try to empower all the children in our pluralistic democracy *must be built on an analysis of the strengths children bring with them to school*

*and take into account the continual nonschool learning of
young people.* This could be called the first principle of educational reconstruction. Applying that principle, it will be
possible to build a program on the strengths of students
rather than assume they are empty vessels waiting to be
filled, or people who because they are young have deficiencies that have to be remediated through schooling. This last
attitude embodies what could be called the deficiency model
of education. Not knowing how to read or to write, for example, are considered deficiencies rather than exciting challenges. I believe this negative attitude toward learning has
contributed significantly to alienating students and to per-
petuating failure in the schools. I remember my son coming
home from first grade and telling me he was stupid because
he couldn't read and a few students in his class could. He
felt deficient rather than challenged by the possibility of
learning. My wife and I had to negate the effect of school
and convince Josh that people were not born knowing how
to read and that he had developed the strength of mind and
language needed to learn.

Analyzing the strengths of students, becoming aware of
what information they have already mastered, is useful in
many ways. Students bring different things with them. Some
come to school reading, others have been exposed to science
or math. Some are handy with tools, others from musical
families might play music or sing. Every class, no matter how
mixed, contains children with enormous strengths, and every
child who has managed to survive and get him- or herself to
school has personal strengths. The more the teachers know
about this the more the students' strengths can be shared,
and the more effectively the educational program can be
fitted to the students. This implies that *every education program must be unique,* must be grounded in the strengths of
the students and recognize and integrate the information
students bring with them to school. Part of the problem of
public education today is that people try to impose a single

system of learning on a singularly diverse people. The goals of public education might be the same everywhere, embodying principles of empowerment and democracy. However, the realization of these principles must uniquely fit the learner's situation. If the first principle of educational reconstruction is *Programs should be built on an analysis of the information children bring with them to school and take into account nonschool learning*, then a second principle is *Each particular educational environment must define its unique way of meeting overall educational goals*. Schools and other places of learning need character. All schools should not look alike or be organized in the same way.

One way to plan a program based on strengths is to develop a strength profile of students, community, and teachers. Of course, it is also possible to compile a deficiency profile. However, as a positive guide to action, working from strengths mobilizes more energy than worrying about deficiencies.

Here's a simple strength profile that analyzes basic skills students bring with them when they come to school.

Strengths students have based on information they received through:

direct observation	language	arts/ expression	culture/ society	science/ technology

If I were to fill in this chart for myself as a five-year-old about to enter school (it makes sense to try this on yourself before projecting yourself into children's worlds), part of my profile might look like this:

DIRECT OBSERVATION

1. Experienced the constant noisy presence of the Lexington Avenue elevated subway. Trains, where they came from and went to, a constant issue.

2. Played on the streets with children of different ages, not accustomed to age segregation.
3. Came from family where everyone worked, so learned to amuse myself by building things, playing fantasy games, and wandering a bit on my own.
4. Lived in a noisy, bustling world and learned to concentrate despite the noise. (The negative aspect of this was that I didn't know much of privacy or silence.)

LANGUAGE

1. Grew up in bilingual environment with grandparents speaking mostly Yiddish, father bilingual in Yiddish and English, mother only speaking English. Speak English, know some Yiddish.
2. Father reads *New York Times* and *Daily Mirror*, Grandfather reads *Daily Forwards*. Know that reading can be left to right or right to left.
3. Live in family with many relatives always present. Lots of storytelling, joking, family history, and legends.

ARTS/EXPRESSION

1. Know Yiddish music-laments, lullabies, freilachs.
2. Know contemporary (1940s) pop music.
3. Play a small accordion.
4. Love to draw, artists in mother's family.

CULTURE/SOCIETY

1. Live in world of Jewish, Irish, Italian cultures.
2. Large families, constant age mixing.
3. Grandparents belong to socialist Yiddish fraternity (Workman's Circle).
4. Grandfather union activist, know a bit about cooperative unionism.
5. Know Yiddish-Jewish culture and rituals.

SCIENCE/TECHNOLOGY

1. Father is a civil engineer who knows about building, I grew up with blueprints and pretend to be able to read them. Make up my own.
2. Grandfather a framer, I am around tools and building equipment and like to use them.
3. Have visited construction jobs and have some (not necessarily accurate) ideas about how buildings get built.

This profile shows some of what I brought to school. My friends had equally interesting strengths. Most of our families were working-class people and we knew of work and culture. For many of us school was a shock. I had reading problems. My teacher said that there was only one way print could run across a page and I didn't believe her from that moment on. My father taught me to read and explained that in school you had to do things the teacher's way. And yet a school program could have been built around our cultural and personal strengths, and knowledge of work and the world. I remember in the fourth or fifth grade building an Indian village of teepees and being afraid to tell the teacher that I could probably build a real house. I also remember learning later on that New York State Indians didn't live in teepees. What if there were some of them in my class — would they have to build the Indian village, too?

Similar profiles could be constructed for analyzing the community a school serves and discovering the strengths of the teachers. I've been struck by how little opportunity teachers have to share skills they have and enjoy using outside of school with their students. They become locked into roles where it either seems inappropriate or too time-consuming to teach what they love to do. I know of a school where several teachers are professional musicians, one an experienced gardener, another a first-rate chess player, and two accomplished watercolorists. Yet that school has no music, chess, or painting program, and no garden. It is a waste of teacher, community, and student resources to deny to schools and communities their unique strengths.

Out of School Learning

In addition to analyzing strength, another factor should be considered when building a new educational program:

How are students accustomed to learning outside of school?

Try to imagine the world of a four-year-old. You have just begun to control language and learned that occasionally infuriating mode called questioning. You can ask about the world and up to a point other people will answer you, usually truthfully. You have time to play, to see how high you can pile blocks before they fall, experiment with a knife and see what it cuts and what it doesn't cut. You also can watch and listen quietly as adults play their lives out before you. There are even occasional short discussions with friends about who owns what toy and how things work. Through *questioning, talking, listening, experimenting,* and *observing* you acquire information about the world. If you are lucky, adults take you places, show you things, explain things about the world. I remember words that my parents and grandparents painfully explained to me as they tried to make their lives and the larger world coherent to me. One was "job," a place where your father and grandfather used tools and built things for other people. The job was where you got money to buy food and clothes and toys. Another word was "museum," a place you visited on Sunday that had fancy and valuable things that it was important to know about even if you didn't particularly like most of them (the medieval armor and weapons were a clear exception).

In addition to the information provided by adults, there is TV and radio. The information provided by these forms is

quick and *chaotic*. There are short ads, continually inter-
rupted stories, episodes, station breaks, news, music, fiction,
all moving continuously. One can't question a TV or radio
program or stop it or review it. The form is linear, and, other
than the opportunity provided by occasional reruns, the information absorbed is partial and fragmented.

The modes of questioning, talking, listening, experimenting, and observing continue throughout life. Teenagers
question each other about issues ranging from sex to the
draft, talk about what they experience or would like to experience, listen to adults very carefully, experiment, especially socially and sexually, and, even though they often try
to conceal it, step back from participation and observe how
things work in the social and material world.

All this may seem obvious. However, once young people
enter school it is usual for questioning to be replaced by
answering, talking by silence, listening by being tested, and
experimenting and observing by following directions. Acquiring information changes from being an open, informal
process of inquiry to a closed, mechanical process involving
memory and obedience. Moreover, the amount of information usually provided in school situations is restricted because of this lack of choice. Here's an example that one of
my daughters encountered in the fifth grade. She was given
this map of the United States in 1826 and was told to use the
map to answer the following six questions:

1. What mountains did people have to cross to reach the frontier? (Appalachian)
2. What two roads on your map cross the Appalachian Mountains? (National and Cumberland)
3. The Cumberland Gap is between what two states? (Kentucky and Tennessee)
4. The Erie Canal was finished in 1826. It started at what river? (Hudson) It ended at what lake? (Erie)
5. The National Road started in what eastern state? (Maryland) It ended in what western state? (Illinois)
6. What river was important to the farmers who lived on the frontier? (Mississippi)

If you can read on a minimal basis you can answer all of the questions without learning anything about life in the 1820s, the Appalachian Mountains, the Erie Canal, or the National Road. The information provided in this exercise (which is just one in a whole series) is null. The content is nonexistent. All you have to do is look at the map and copy what you see. There is nothing to learn but the mechanical procedure of matching. In question five, for example, if you know where east is, where west is, and can read the words *National Road,* you can get the answer right and know no more than you began with. In fact, my daughter and her friends never even bothered to memorize any of the answers to questions like these because they knew that as long as the map was there the answer was on the page. They learned a mechanical procedure for getting correct answers.

The purple ditto master had one final question that illustrates a sophisticated version of the mechanical mode of dealing with information:

> Imagine that someone living today could ask you this question. How would you answer back? "The frontier is a lonely, wild place. Why do you want to live there?"

"Why?" indeed. My daughter Erica's answer was "I wouldn't want to live there." She should have said "it provided opportunity," "there was cheap land," and the other pronouncements that her textbook made. She was marked wrong, yet how many people who went to settle the frontier wanted to go there and how many went because of poverty, oppression, curiosity, or ignorance of the wildness and loneliness? Erica's answer could lead to an interesting analysis of the settling of the American continent, but the question as phrased closed things down and made her wrong.

There probably is a place for learning how to answer closed questions in a mechanical way. However, a principle of educational reconstruction, based on the belief that children will be empowered if they are allowed to exercise their strengths, should be that *questioning, talking, listening, experimenting, and observing should be considered central ways to acquire basic skills and encouraged in learning situations.* The modes children use naturally and informally outside of school should provide a base for acquiring more complex information and for developing more sophisticated means of organizing information.

Content and Censorship

Another central concern for revitalizing education is:

What content should be provided by a public education program and what techniques for acquiring and organizing this content should be demonstrated and taught?

This question raises the problems of *content* and *censorship,* which have been central to debates over basic skills over the past 200 years. An obvious example and one I believe still has major negative consequences these days took place during the cold war in the late forties and early fifties. Communists were prohibited from talking and teaching in public schools. In addition, intelligent discussions of communism, socialism, syndicalism, and other noncapitalist forms of social and economic organization disappeared from the classroom. As a result, people graduate from high school with inadequate information about the social forms that the majority of the world lives under. Moreover, by being ignorant of other social forms, they are deprived of ideas that may be useful in solving our own problems. Here is a clear case of information deficiency that can lead to closing options to citizens of our supposed democracy. The United States is the only nonfascist nation I can think of without a major socialist or social democratic party, and the schools have played their part in depriving citizens of knowledge of socialist options that are compatible with democracy, though these options exist throughout Europe in the nations that are supposedly our closest allies.

There are other major content struggles that focus on the schools. Energy development is a crucial social issue in our society. The energy corporations provide hundreds of thousands of copies of books that are given away free in the public schools. They range all the way from Exxon's *Mickey Mouse and Goofy Explore Energy*, which, under the guise of an objective analysis of future fuel sources, advocates nuclear energy, to Westinghouse Electric's booklet *For a Mature Audience Only*, which ends

> The switch to coal and nuclear fuel won't happen overnight. Each of us, however, can help make it happen. By informing our families, neighbors, friends, and legislators of the realistic energy picture, *you* can make it happen.[46]

The first sentence assumes conversion will happen, the third that a realistic energy picture is what "you" somehow got from the booklet and that students therefore should lobby for Westinghouse.

In a community I visited, there has been a struggle over whether to support or oppose oil drilling on- and offshore just north of town. At the time people were debating this issue, a number of corporate energy booklets (most in comic-book form) were distributed free to all the children at school. At the same time, some local opponents of oil development were prohibited from making presentations in school on the ground that they were not neutral. It took a lot of analysis and argument to convince teachers and the school board that the material from the oil company was not neutral either. This is another example of information deprivation in school.

The response of several teachers and board members to arguments about the biased nature of presentations about energy development was to pull the old strategy of calling for "back to basics," for a curriculum without content at all, one that *just* dealt with skills. The problem with that choice was that in trying to eliminate all information, the problem of motivation was created. If there was nothing interesting to read there was no reason to read. That implied that many children would have to be coerced to read, which in turn implied that strict discipline or a behavioral reward system had to be adopted. This in turn implied that students were not to be encouraged to ask questions and explore the adult world. By trying to eliminate content, a philosophy of obedience had to be adopted, one that advocated accepting the status quo and, therefore, tacitly supported the position of the oil companies. Fortunately, things never got that far. The other option, presenting students with information from both sides and letting them make up their own minds as befits members of a democracy, is currently being explored.

There is no way to eliminate content from an educational program without replacing it by some system of coercion. In a program that advocates thought and aspires to democracy, the *enrichment of content* is a major goal. A principle emerging from this could be stated: *Content is central and many views should be presented when dealing with any issue.* Welcome divergent views and make them explicit. Don't be afraid of any view but put it directly next to opposing views. Teachers should trust their pupils to sort things out and help them develop techniques for dealing with information, and help them learn to analyze a situation in order to discover *what information is lacking in order to develop a rounded picture of what they are studying.*

Building a List of Priorities

It is important to develop a general plan for reconstructing public education in your community before trying to institute specific changes. The plan should come from an analysis of current educational financial practice, take into account the strengths of your children and your community, be open to out-of-school learning, and unafraid of incorporating controversial ideas.

I find it useful, while constructing a program for change, to measure all of my proposals against the fundamental notion that public education exists as part of our struggle to create democracy. With this underlying principle, it is possible to come up with suggestions for minor as well as major changes with the knowledge that they are all governed by a central, overall idea. It is also possible, once a plan is articulated, to sort out priorities and begin to act with the knowledge that each small change is actually part of the larger goal of building a system of public education that contributes to the development of democracy in our nation.

My Priorities for Change

I will conclude with my list of a half dozen specific things to do now. You should create your own list based on the resources of your community and an analysis of the strengths and weaknesses of the school you want to change.

1. It is essential to oppose the tyranny of testing, to eliminate the equation of teaching with testing, and to undermine the notion that test performances can provide an objective measure of intelligence and ability. If we can achieve this, the way will be open for teachers to teach once more and for interesting content and thoughtful learning to take place.

It is essential that people understand that standardized tests, though they do not yield useful assessments of what individual children do, have other effects on children and schools. A pamphlet put out by the North Dakota Study Group on Testing describes some of the pernicious effects of the use of standardized tests:

1. They often determine children's future class placement and classification (slow, bright).
2. They put pressure on teachers to spend large portions of time coaching children for the tests — trying to outwit the test makers.
3. They affect the curriculum, the skills, and the values of the school, since teachers will often shape the school day to fit the tests, not the children.

4. Large sums of money are given to schools to improve their reading programs. The success of these programs is often determined by test scores.

5. Children judge themselves by how they do on the tests. They assume that test questions are what reading "is all about."

6. Parents, not having seen the tests, often judge their children by their test scores, too.[47]

Accepting all these negative consequences of standardized tests does not mean that there is no need to assess anything in school. What we need are fair, educationally useful means of assessing individual achievement. It is crucial to realize that *rejecting standardized tests is not the same as having no standards.* Standards can and must be set by parents, teachers, and other educators. And children must be fairly assessed, on an individual basis if necessary, to see how they are doing. There are alternative means of assessment available, which range from individual student profiles to tests carefully designed to be free of bias. We should directly attack the myth of standardized testing and ask the question of whether the tests themselves haven't contributed to the lowering of standards in the school, and the demoralization of students and teachers.

2. On a positive note, I believe an important thing we can do easily and quickly is reestablish the importance of student speech and open-ended discussion in school. Comprehension and content should be a major focus for revitalization of the schools. Teachers should be encouraged to devote time to listening to their students. Community people should be invited into schools to discuss current issues. Debates, storytelling, discussion and critical analysis of films and books, should replace textbook questions and test taking. Intelligent conversation, improvisation, well-thought-out questioning, can and should be woven into all of the subjects taught at school.

One concrete way to initiate this change might be to establish a student publishing guild at the school and purchase a small printing press. Writing, discussing, and printing articles of current interest, making editorial decisions, and discussing the quality of student work can lead to the development of intelligent speech and the careful use of language in all areas of the curriculum. I am currently working with one public school that is attempting such a program. We have a small handpress as well as the use of an offset press that we share with other schools. At present we are planning a science newsletter, a literary magazine, and several small volumes of poetry and fiction, as well as several oral history interviews and fictional portraits of historical figures. We are also thinking of extending the program to include student-developed math texts, and a small student-run printing business to support student projects.

The presence of the press has led to conversation dealing not merely with its use but with the content of what should be printed and, by extension, of what is learned. Sometimes a small change, like buying a press, can lead to other more fundamental changes.

3. *Another priority is the acknowledgment of the arts as basic skills.* Whether through the development of centers of expression or through changes on a school or local level, arts programs should be established and given the same status as language, mathematics, and science programs. Not every school can manage to cover all the arts from music to filmmaking, but not every literary genre can be covered in English either. One must choose one's art program carefully, balancing community desires with staff talent and community resources, and then make a major commitment to develop and support a locally designed program. One school might choose music and dance with lesser emphasis on the visual arts, while another might choose painting, drawing, sculpture, and woodcarving. These selective emphases are necessary short of having comprehensive art centers, just as

the choice of books is necessary in language and the choice of period and location to study is necessary in history.

What is probably going to be the greatest problem in developing these programs is getting people to think of art as basic to decent public education. The art-as-frills mentality has to be confronted directly and we have to insist that the skills and the pleasures derived from the arts not be reserved for a privileged few but be owed to all children.

4. Another priority, one which is also not difficult to achieve (and certainly not expensive), is to bring people from the community into the schools and get students into the community. This flow in and out of the school should not be confused with a one-time visit or a talk or lecture. Schools should be invited to use the resources of the community to enrich their programs, and people with skills should be encouraged to share them with young people.

One way to develop a program like this is to have several classes work on a community resources questionnaire, and then have the students go out into the community and do all the interviewing and compiling of data themselves. Simply doing the interviews is a way to initiate student mobility. Moreover, many community people might find it harder to refuse a student request for participation than to refuse one that came through official channels.

The development of community learning programs can have the additional benefit of enriching the content of what is offered to students. It can give them a feel for many more possibilities for themselves as adults than can any commercially produced program on vocational choice.

5. Health and nutrition are major concerns in our society and in the schools. The development of a comfortable lunchroom and a school garden as part of a comprehensive nutrition program is also a priority. The school-lunch program is a disaster in just about every public school, and the improvement of food quality and service can mobilize a wide range of parents and teachers.

I believe in the decentralization of food services. Schools should have their own cooking facilities and students should play major roles in the purchase, growing, preparing, and serving of food. They should learn to cook, prepare menus, take turns cleaning, be involved in deciding ways to make the lunchroom attractive, and deal with outrageous student behavior. The lunchroom can be a model of a small, democratically run cooperative business. It can also be a center for the study of diet and its effect on behavior.

This, along with a small health clinic run by students and paraprofessionals, could be starting points for the revitalization of individual schools. The central concern, however, has to be with giving students an actual voice in what happens as well as a responsibility for the consequences of their decisions.

6. *A final priority for me is the development of a program dealing with the use of tools, and with learning how to use and control the tools of contemporary technology.* If I could, I'd probably build a program using a carpenter's toolbox and a home computer. How could they be used? How do they relate to each other? What can one build and what can the other do? What project could be developed that could be planned by computer and built with the tools we have? How can we get the materials needed and when will we begin to work?

An understanding of technology — the effect it has on our lives and the social responsibility of having such powerful tools — is essential for our citizens. The ability to use tools oneself is equally essential. A reconstructed science program from kindergarten up is one of my priorities.

There are many other ways to take first steps once a commitment is made to the revitalization of public education. All involve imagination, intelligence, and the ability to develop and articulate a plan, that is, to use the basic skills of democratic functioning too infrequently taught in schools.

Underlying our plans has to be a commitment to democracy, to education for all the children of all the people. Specific changes are only that, beginning points in what will certainly be a long struggle, not merely to make the schools places where young people learn to function democratically, but to make our society one in which adults can function democratically.

This raises one last question, an as-yet-unanswerable question. What can the schools contribute to the development of democracy in the United States? What can and will we do for our children and alongside our children to revitalize those ideas that define our greatness — the ideas that all people can live decent lives; that all children should have the opportunity to grow healthy and fulfill their potential; and finally, the idea that a nation can be built of citizens who have control over their lives and at the same time care about the lives of all other citizens?

·APPENDIX I·

On Testing

SIR FRANCIS GALTON, in his book *Hereditary Genius,* published in 1869, hypothesized that intelligence could be measured and, moreover, that its distribution among a nation's population could be represented as a normal curve. This meant that most people were average, with a small number of inferior and superior intelligences. Galton's imaginary scale was converted into a test for intelligence by the Frenchman Alfred Binet. He constructed a series of tests designed to sort out people in a way that would produce a normal curve.

Binet's test was published in 1908 and was refined and reworked in the United States by Terman and Simon, Thorndike, and others. Binet's test was for individuals. Group tests and tests for achievement in academic subjects were developed during the first two decades of the twentieth century.

The first standardized test of school children's achievement was constructed in 1910 by the psychologist Edward Thorndike, who was a professor at Teachers College, Columbia. It was a test of handwriting. Thorndike collected over 20,000 samples of handwriting by fifth through eighth graders. He also selected about fifty people whom he considered expert judges of handwriting and gave them samples to rank in order of excellence, from one to ten. He assumed that it was possible to make this ranking and set up standards of excellence that make one wonder about the whole business of ranking. Here is a sample of the standards that emerged, standards that he felt could be refined even more to provide an exact measure of the quality of handwriting:[48]

1. seated on the
curb was my
driver and

2. bushes and the carriage
swayed along down the
driveway. ye andre

3. gathering about them melted away in an instant leaving
only a poor old lady

4. card, John vanished behind the
bushes and the carriage moved

5. moved along down the driveway. The
audience of passers by which had
been
gathering about them melted away

   Then the carelessly gentleman stepped lightly into Warrens carriage and
   held out a small card, John vanished behind the bushes and the carriage moved

6. Then the carelessly dressed gentlemen
   stepped lightly into Warrens carriage and
   held out a small card, John vanished behind the

   by which had been gathering about them melted away in an instant leaving only a poor
   old lady on the curb. Albert was sadly

   Then the carelessly dressed gentleman
   stepped lightly into Warren's carriage moved
   and held out a small card, John vanished

7. driveway. The audience of passers-by, which
had been gathering about them melted away
in an instant leaving only a poor old lady on
the curb. Albert was sadly striding

8. riage moved along down the
driveway. The audience of passers-by which had been gathering about them melted away

along the down the driveway
The audience of passers-by which
had been gathering about them

John vanished behind the
bushes and the carriage
moved along down the
driveway The audience

9. lightly into Warren's carriage and held out a
small card, John vanished behind the bushes
and the carriage moved along down the drive-

behind the bushes and the carriage moved
along down the driveway. The audience
of passers-by

Then the carelessly dressed gentleman stepped
lightly into Warren's carriage and held out a small
card, John vanished behind the bushes and the

10. Then the carelessly dressed gentleman stepped
lightly into Warren's carriage and held out a
ished behind the bushes and the carriage moved along down the driveway.
The audience of passers-by which had

Then the carelessly dressed gentleman
stepped lightly into Warren's carriage and

Then the carelessly dressed
gentlemen stepped lightly
into Warren's carriage and

Certainly there's a contrast between one and ten, and even between, say, one to three, four to six, and seven to ten. But by the time one gets to differentiating between handwriting in categories seven to ten, things become a bit scholastic. Are slanted o's better than upright o's? Is an open, flowing hand any less legible than an angular one? One gets the feeling that distinctions are being manufactured.

Once a test is created, however, the mischief begins. Because handwriting can now be measured, the schools must teach to level ten rather than help each student develop a legible, fluid style of writing. Handwriting textbooks were created to conform to Thorndike's standards. How many of us remember the torture of handwriting classes in which we were judged by the approximation of our efforts to the "standard" of excellent writing? I was a constant B—, though I believe my level-seven handwriting is quite legible and reflects my character more than the narrow, slanted, more formal script of level ten.

In addition to Thorndike's work on handwriting, standards for English composition and arithmetic were also being worked on during the 1910s. Embodied in these early efforts was the idea that intelligence and academic achievement could somehow be related, and that every subject must have a unique hierarchical structure ranging in discrete steps from simple to complex. In terms of performance, this meant creating rankings from inadequate to excellent. The idea that there might be many forms of excellence or that in subjects like handwriting and writing there were no single standards of excellence was not entertained so far as I can tell.

Great impetus was given to the test-making and test-giving industry during World War I when the United States Army adopted a series of group tests to decide who was fit for service, and who should be channeled to menial and grunt labor and who should be sent to officers training school.

From September 1917 to January 1919, the army tested 1,726,966 people, including all men called up in the white draft and colored draft (there were two separate drafts into the segregated army) as well as 42,000 commissioned officers. Individual examinations were given to 82,500 men. Thus began the enormous growth of the educational-psychology business and the testing industry with its anti-democratic bias.

The results of the army tests are fascinating. The tests show officers to be superior in intelligence, whites to be superior to blacks, middle-class men to be superior to poor whites. Therefore, the tests served to channel poor and black men into the grunt roles, and channel the educated, white, middle-class men into command and skill roles. Of course, the test makers and test givers were educated, white, middle-class men who wrote the test from the perspective of their worlds, though this was not considered a biasing factor. One underlying assumption, for example, is that excellence in reading, writing, and other school-related skills was a good predictor of leadership. Yet, I wonder whether a straight-A college student would be a better leader of soldiers than a person with no formal education but fifteen years experience leading a construction gang.

In the same book that discusses the results of the army testing, the author, Rudolf Pintner, confidently claims of other testing that

> all results show the negro [sic] decidedly inferior to the white on standard intelligence tests. These results are sufficiently numerous and consistent to point to a racial difference in intelligence. The overlapping of the two races is great, and the most liberal estimate seems to be that at most 25% of the colored reach or exceed the median intelligence of the whites.[49]

Notice the leap that Pintner makes from performance on certain tests to statements about intelligence per se. That is a leap of faith in the tests that has not stood up. Many of the results he based his conclusions on have subsequently been proved to have been falsified, and the tests themselves shown to be inadequate and biased.

It may be that these class- and racebound results of tests were not built into the tests and surprised the testmakers. However, there is some evidence that bias was intentionally built into early tests. W. E. B. DuBois, in a 1925 issue of *Crisis,* mentions that a battery of achievement tests were given to blacks and whites in Louisville. The blacks did as well as the whites and, therefore, the results were embarrassing to the whites. The tests were withdrawn and "renormed," a euphemism for saying *readjusted* so the results would come out right.[50]

Another specific instance of setting norms as a social and political act was described in a recent issue of the *History of Education Quarterly* (Vol. 19, #3, Fall '79, p. 289). It seems that in 1919, Columbia University was worried about having too many Jewish students. They therefore adopted the Tests for Mental Alertness devised by E. L. Thorndike of Teachers College, the man who developed the handwriting test, partly on the assumption that "objectionable" applicants would not have "had the home experiences which enable them to pass these tests as successfully as the average American boy." They succeeded at least temporarily in lowering Jewish admissions.[51]

Given this background, it makes sense to take a closer look at the contents of standardized tests, keeping in mind that the test maker is a person with particular biases and intentions, and that norms are not objective phenomena but invented standards that relate to class and culture. A good way to study tests is to begin by taking one yourself. Try this short one:

INSTRUCTIONS: For questions 1 to 3, read the word enclosed in the arrow. Then put an X on the word next to the arrow that is *most* similar in meaning to the word in the arrow.

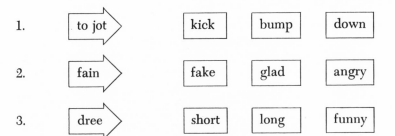

1. to jot | kick | bump | down
2. fain | fake | glad | angry
3. dree | short | long | funny

DIRECTIONS: For questions 4 to 6, look at the picture and complete the sentence that *best* describes the picture.

4. The girl is
   a) happy
   b) grateful
   c) generous

5. The man is
   a) hungry
   b) angry
   c) jealous

6. The people are
   a) in the fields
   b) on a picnic
   c) in school

INSTRUCTIONS: For question 7, look at the picture and pick out the title that best fits the picture.

7. The best name for this picture is
   a) Sad Child
   b) Waiting
   c) The Pacifier

Here are the answers to the test questions:

Question 1: The answer is *bump*. The word *down* was one of the choices to trick you through associating *jot* with *jot down;* the word *kick* was made a choice because it was close enough in mode to *bump* to make a guess between *kick* and *bump* difficult. The choices were set up to trick you, not test whether you read the words. If you had fluent command of sixteenth-century English, you'd have no trouble with this question. If not, you might be able to read all the words and still get the wrong answer.

Question 2: The answer is *glad,* as in "I fain would help thee," a not-uncommon sentence in Shakespearean and other Elizabethan theater. If you were lucky enough to be exposed to Shakespeare, you could probably make a correct intelligent guess. If not, *fain* might, through sound association (*f*'s), lead you to choose *fake,* or through your anger at not having the slightest idea what the word *fain* means even though you can read it perfectly well, to choose *angry*. This item tests your cultural background and is biased toward people who've been exposed to Elizabethan language and culture.

Question 3: Dree is Scottish for something long and drawn out or tedious. If your standard dialect was Scots or Northumbrian you'd have no trouble with this question. If you could read the question and spoke some other standard dialect of English, your chances of getting the question right would be one in three. This is what is meant when some people criticize standard tests as being linguistically biased.

Question 4: The girl is happy and generous, but the right answer is grateful. The directions say find the answer that fits best and the maker of the test (in this case, me) decided that grateful was the best fit. The reason was not arbitrary, as the caption of this picture from the People's Republic of China is "Thanks People's Liberation Army for helping with the harvest." If you look closely you'll notice several army hats and knapsacks on the ground in the lower left-hand corner. If you were Chinese you'd know they were from soldiers who had come to help the populace. If you weren't Chinese you might think they represented an invading army or a wartime situation. You also might not even notice them. This question is culturally biased. You might be able to read and know the meaning of *happy, grateful,* and *generous* and still get the answer wrong.

Question 5: Here the question of best fit comes up again. This picture of Saturn devouring his son shows an angry, hungry man. However, if you knew the legend of Saturn's attempt to devour his children, you'd know that the fit the tester was looking for was "jealous." This question doesn't test your ability to read or know all the words in the question. It tests your knowledge of Greek mythology. If you happened to grow up in a home where your parents read Greek myths to the children, or if you went to a school that taught mythology, you'd have a good chance of getting the answer correct.

Question 6: The people are in the fields, and have had a picnic. However, they are in school. The man with grain in his hand (and with a blue Mao jacket and red undershirt) is the teacher, and the rest of the children and adults are the students. This school doesn't look anything like our schools, and unless you knew something about education in China, "school" would be the least likely of the three choices. However, many people get this question right because they are looking for a trick question. "Picnic" seems too obvious and fits better than in the fields. But by the time they are in the middle of this (and other achievement tests), they are no longer looking for obvious answers as they expect to be tricked. When tests set you up to be tricked they often fail to reveal what you know.

Question 7: The three choices fit equally well, and Chaim Soutine, the painter, simply called the picture "Child." It's up to the tester to pick a best fit and to the tested to make a lucky guess. On every test there's likely to be a few items like this that depend solely on the whim of the test maker.

It is important to realize that someone who could read every word on this test could fail miserably because they knew nothing about mythology or English literature. The test is clearly biased toward people with certain awareness that has nothing to do with reading. It is unfair. In fact it was consciously constructed to be unfair. I don't know how much conscious bias is built into the standard tests given to our children. However, the cultural and linguistic suppositions that I parodied in my test can be found in every standardized test of reading. Here are just a few samples of unfair questions taken from recent versions of the California Test of Basic Skills and the Stanford Achievement Tests:

ITEM 1:

A CINDER is a piece of . . . □ rock □ sand □ burned coal □ fire brick

We have cinders in our wood stove but my children have never seen coal. We also used cinder blocks in building a wall. What would a correct answer be for them? And if they got the wrong answer, would it mean they couldn't read the words in the question?

ITEM 2:

One child read the question correctly and put an X on the boy. The other put an X on the car. The first child's reason was that the boy was walking toward the car and since the car was empty it couldn't be going for a ride. The other boy's answer was that you had to have a car to go for a ride. They both read the question correctly and understood it. One was "right" and the other "wrong."

ITEM 3:

READ THIS:

> Since he first thought about those things, George wanted to be an engineer. It was said that his Great-Grandfather Green had had something to do with the Panama Canal. His Grandfather Walsh had planned the first large group of look-alike houses in their town. One of the streets was named for George's grandfather. And his own father spent a great deal of time away from home "estimating" — he would study what would be needed to build a new dam or bridge or road and tell his company what it would cost.

Which shows the kind of houses Grandfather Walsh planned?

One child marked the identical suburban homes, another marked the identical tenements. Which is right? Which one reads better? In many urban areas houses have many stories and in the neighborhood I taught in the "first large look-alike houses in the town" were in a twenty-story Federal housing project. This is a subtle example of the kind of culture bias that pervades many tests.

Item 4:

> An architect's most important tools are his —
>   Ⓔ   pencil and paper
>   Ⓕ   buildings
>   Ⓖ   ideas
>   Ⓗ   bricks

The test maker decided that the best fit here was G, Ideas. Many students (and adults as well) answer E, pencil and paper, arguing that ideas are not, properly speaking, tools. Which read better?

Item 5:

Here's a page from *Reading Tests: Do They Help or Hurt Your Child?*, published by the North Dakota Study Group on Testing, along with some of the author's comments. Notice that the answer to the first question requires some knowledge of science and the second some knowledge of mythology. To get the correct answers, being able to read, which is what the test is supposed to evaluate, is not enough.

Ants are found in almost all parts of the world, and they are the most common insects on earth. Although many ants are hard workers, others do no work at all. One *kind* of ant that does not work is the Amazon ant. Amazon ants are fierce fighters, but they cannot dig their own nests or even feed themselves. They actually have slaves to do these things for them. The slaves, another kind of ant, are captured in battle by the Amazons.

You can suppose that without slaves Amazon ants would —

    Ⓐ   go to work
    Ⓑ   run away
    Ⓒ   make nests
    Ⓓ   die

According to legend, there were people known as Amazons. They probably —

Ⓐ were warriors
Ⓑ couldn't feed themselves
Ⓒ were strong workers
Ⓓ were found in all parts of the world

Do the tests require special knowledge?

These tests are given to your children to find out if they can read. . . . Not to determine if they know about specific topics or have learned particular facts. Yet, finding the answer to the first question here requires scientific knowledge.

Many children who read well would answer by saying that ants, like people, would soon learn to go to work if they didn't have slaves. However, the correct answer is *die.*

For the second question, where we are meant to assume that ants *are* like people, several of the answers seem equally sensible, unless the child *already* knows that the Amazons of ancient legend were warriors.[52]

I could give many more examples from any standardized reading test. It is more important that parents and teachers examine the tests themselves and think about whether they measure what they claim to measure.

Standardized tests, though they do not yield useful assessments of what individual children do, have other effects on children and schools. As the North Dakota Study Group's pamphlet says, the effects of standardized testing are many:

1. They often determine children's future class placement and classification (slow, bright).
2. They put pressure on teachers to spend large portions of time coaching children for the tests — trying to outwit the test makers.
3. They affect the curriculum, the skills, and the values of the school, since teachers will often shape the school day to fit the tests, not the children.
4. Large sums of money are given to schools to improve their reading programs. The success of these programs is often determined by test scores.

5. Children judge themselves by how they do on the tests. They assume that test questions are what reading "is all about."
6. Parents, not having seen the tests, often judge their children by their test scores, too.[53]

Accepting all these negative consequences of standardized tests does not mean that there is no need to assess anything in school. What we need are fair, educationally useful means of assessing individual achievement. It is crucial to develop and maintain standards which can and must be set by parents, teachers, and other educators. And children must be fairly assessed, on an individual basis if necessary, to see how they are doing. There are alternative means of assessment available, which range from individual student profiles to tests carefully designed to be free of bias. We should directly attack the myth of standardized testing and open the questions of whether the tests themselves haven't contributed to the lowering of standards in the schools.

Notes

—

1. Shraag and Divoki, *The Myth of the Hyperactive Child* (1976).
2. Fast, *Citizen Tom Paine* (1943), unpaged.
3. Bowen, *Writing of Biography* (1951), p. 8.
4. Bowen, *The Most Dangerous Man in America* (1974), p. 64.
5. Franklin, *Proposals Relating to the Education of Youth in Pennsylvania* (1749), unpaged.
6. Ibid.
7. Stowe, *The Report on Elementary Public Instruction in Europe* (1837), p. 2.
8. Ibid., p. 3.
9. Von Marenholz-Bulow, *Reminiscences of Friedrich Froebel* (1877), p. 67.
10. Wallace, *Rockdale* (1978). A marvelous account of the growth of an American village in the early Industrial Revolution. The author describes the book as "an account of the coming of the machines, the making of a new way of life in the mill hamlets, the triumph of evangelical capitalists over socialists and infidels, and the transformation of the workers into Christian soldiers in a cotton manufacturing district in Pennsylvania in the years before and during the Civil War."
11. Von Marenholz-Bulow, *Reminiscences*, p. 200.
12. *First Century of National Existence: The United States as They Were and Are* (1872), p. 384.
13. Cremin, *The Transformation of the School* (1961), p. 129.
14. Ibid., pp. 129–130.
15. Parker, *Talks on Pedagogics* (1894).
16. Rice, *The Public School System of the United States* (1893).
17. Nearing, *The New Education* (1915), p. 18.
18. McCaul, "Dewey's Chicago," *The School Review* (Summer 1959), pp. 258–281.
19. Dewey, *My Pedagogic Creed* (1897), p. 16.
20. Dewey and Dewey, *Schools of Tomorrow* (1915), p. 313.

21. Patri, *A Schoolmaster of the Great City* (1923), p. 9.
22. Ibid., p. 13.
23. Ibid., p. 211.
24. This quotation appeared in Woodhull, "The Aims and Methods of Science Teaching," *General Science Quarterly*, volume 2 (November 1917), p. 249. I attributed it to Alice for the sake of my story.
25. Proceedings of the N.E.A. meeting in Oakland, California (1923), pp. 180–188.
26. Ibid., pp. 168–176.
27. Charters, *Journal of Home Economics*, volume 10 (March 1918), p. 117.
28. Rugg, *America's March Toward Democracy* (1937). The Rugg textbook controversy was the subject of an entire issue of *Propaganda Analysis*, volume 4, number 4 (February 25, 1941). This, as well as the Rugg texts themselves, have been main sources for my reconstruction of the Rugg controversy in Turin. Here is a quote from *Propaganda Analysis* (p. 7) that describes the controversy:

Probably the hardest attack of the early months of the current fight, in 1939, was that of the American Federation of Advertisers. This was based at first on the treatment of advertising in Dr. Rugg's *Introduction to the Problems of American Culture*. It was quickly taken up by other advertising groups, and by the bulletin of the American Newspaper Publishers Association. Then the attack was broadened and the whole Rugg series came to be condemned as subversive. The basis for this view was laid in a report by Alfred T. Falk, director of the Advertising Federation's Bureau of Research and Education, called "The Rugg Technique of Indoctrination." The report examined Dr. Rugg's philosophy of social reconstruction as expressed in his adult discussion book, *The Great Technology*.

"This fantastic panacea," Mr. Falk says, "attempts to graft the tenets of technocracy upon a framework of Marxian socialism." Taking Dr. Rugg's statement that "A new public mind is to be created," Mr. Falk attempted to show that the tetxbooks worked toward this end by an "approach . . . of stealth." There are four steps in the Rugg indoctrination, Mr. Falk says. "First, the child is taught the great principle of Change — everything is in a constant state of change and we must expect all institutions to be changed in the future, especially forms of government and social organization. Second, the student is shown by numerous examples of factual and fictitious evidence that our present situation in this country is very unsatisfactory and our system has worked badly. Third, the child is disillusioned of any preconceived ideas that America has a glorious history or that the founding fathers were men of good intent. Rather, it is shown that our form of society was designed to benefit only the minority ruling class. Fourth, the panacea of social reconstruction and collectivist planning is advanced as the inevitable coming change.

As one of Rugg's "unrepresentative examples," Mr. Falk quotes this passage from the textbook, *Conquests of America* (p. 540), in a reference to mill wages: "These people did not want to go to the towns to work in factories because the wages there were poor indeed — fifty hours a week for $5 . . ."

29. Scott, Hill, and Burns, eds., *The Great Debate* (1959), p. 57.
30. The *San Francisco Chronicle*, January 30, 1981.
31. *First Century*, p. 352.
32. Wesker, *Words as Definitions of Experience* (1976), p. 4.
33. Ibid., p. 5.
34. Ibid., pp. 14, 15.
35. Dewey, *John Dewey on Education: Selected Writings* (1974), p. 351.
36. Marietta Johnson's work is described in Johnson, *Thirty Years with an Idea* (1974). Sybil Marshall's work is described in Marshall, *An Experiment in Education* (1963). The Walden School in New Lincoln is described in Cremin, *Transformation*.
37. Gross, *The Lifelong Learner* (1977), pp. 15–16.
38. Mortensen, *Schools for Life* (1977), p. 9.
39. The idea of well-played games is beautifully elaborated in de Koven, *The Well-Played Game* (1978).
40. Branan and Nathan, *Learning Magazine* (March 1977).
41. Norris School Co-op Program, *Adult Education*, volume 10, number 4 (June 1938).
42. Sonorov and Kahn, *You and Your Community: A Primer* (1944).
43. Ibid.
44. Berkeley Citizens' Masterplan Facilities Committee, Berkeley Unified School District (June 15, 1978).
45. Ayres, *The Cleveland School Survey*, volume 24 (1916), p. 75.
46. Harty, *Hucksters in the Classroom: A Review of Industry Propaganda in Schools* (1979), p. 83.
47. North Dakota Study Group on Evaluation, *Reading Tests: Do They Help or Hurt Your Child.*
48. Thorndike, *Handwriting* (1917). In all fairness to Thorndike, he did not try to relate handwriting to intelligence. In fact, in his monograph describing the handwriting test, he said that at a certain point it would be better to learn to use a typewriter than to attempt to improve handwriting.

49. Pintner, *Intelligence Testing: Methods and Results* (1923), p. 345.
50. Du Bois, *Crisis*, volume 40 (1925).
51. Synnott, "The Admission and Arsenal of Minority Students at Harvard, Yale and Princeton 1900–1950," *Journal of the History of Education*, volume 19, number 3 (Fall 1979), p. 289.
52. North Dakota Study Group, *Reading Tests*.
53. Ibid.

Bibliography

Background for the history of education in Turin as well as for many of the ideas expressed throughout the book emerged from reading and research on our educational past that I've been doing over the last three years. Without the help of Cynthia Brown, with her love of libraries and intuition about the location of original sources, the historical work on this book would not have been possible. And without the generous donation by Louis Laub of two hundred volumes of American educational classics to the Coastal Ridge Center, where I work, it would have been impossible for me to have immediate access to historical sources and to be able to reread, cross reference, and internalize aspects of educational history. In particular, the donation of the United States Commissioner of Education's reports from 1876 to 1901 as well as the proceedings of the National Education Association from 1923 to 1951 were invaluable sources of educational thought and debate. Paul Monroe's five volume *Cyclopedia of Education* (published by Macmillan from 1910 to 1914) was another major source that I relied on. In fact, it was by reading the article on Ohio Education in the Cyclopedia that I discovered Calvin Stowe and Henry Beecher's work in Cincinnati.

Another book that was a central source of information and leads is entitled *First Century of National Existence: The United States as They Were and Are. First Century* was compiled, as the front page indicates, by "an eminent Corps of Scientific and Literary Men" and published by L. Stebbins of Hartford, Connecticut, in 1872. The book is a celebration of and reflection on the first hundred years of our national existence. The section on education, which is over one hundred double-column pages long, was written by Henry Barnard, who was to become the first United States Commissioner of Education. In compiling his information on one hundred years of education in the United States, Barnard sent out requests to over one hundred prominent educators and scholars that they write him about their own educational experiences and their feelings about progress in public education. The responses from people ranging from Noah Webster to Peter Parley (who wrote the first illustrated geography book) are lively and personal and convey a sense of the struggle for public education from 1800 to 1872.

These sources, as well as Lawrence Cremin's *Transformation of the Schools*, led me to many other sources as I followed footnoted references or names or events mentioned casually.

Here is the bibliography of my sources:

Ayres, Leonard P. *The Cleveland School Survey.* 26 vols. Cleveland, Ohio: The Survey Committee of the Cleveland Foundation, 1915–1917.

Bailyn, Bernard. *Education in the Forming of American Society.* New York: Vintage Books, 1960.

Ballard, Philip Boswood. *The Changing School.* London: Hodder and Stoughton, 1926.

Berkeley Citizens' Masterplan Facilities Committee, Berkeley Unified School District (June 15, 1978).

Bowen, Catherine Drinker. *The Most Dangerous Man in America.* Boston: Atlantic–Little, Brown, 1974.

———. *Writing of Biography.* Boston: The Writer, 1951.

Bowers, C. A. *The Progressive Educator and the Depression.* New York: Random House, 1969.

Branan, Karen, and Nathan, Joe. "Students as Consumer Advocates." *Learning Magazine* (March 1977).

Charters, W. W. "The Project Method of Learning." *Journal of Home Economics* 10 (March 1918): 168–178.

Cobb, Stanwood. *The New Leaven: Progressive Education and Its Effect upon the Child and Society.* New York: Arno Press and the *New York Times*, 1969. Originally published in New York by the John Day Company in 1932.

Cremin, Lawrence A. *Public Education.* New York: Basic Books, 1976.

———. *Traditions of American Education.* New York: Basic Books, 1977.

———. *The Transformation of the School: Progressivism in American Education, 1876–1957.* New York: Alfred A. Knopf, 1961.

De Guimps, Roger. *Pestalozzi: His Life and Work.* International Education Series. New York: D. Appleton and Company, 1894.

De Koven, Bernard. *The Well-Played Game.* New York: Doubleday, 1978.

Dennison, George. *The Lives of Children.* New York: Bantam Books, 1968.

Dewey, John. *The Child and the Curriculum and the School and Society.* Introduction by Leonard Carmichael. Chicago and London: The University of Chicago Press, 1971.

————. *Education Today.* Edited by Joseph Ratner. New York: G.P. Putnam's Sons, 1940.

————. *Experience and Education.* The Kappa Delta Pi Lecture Series. New York: Collier Books, 1963.

————. *John Dewey on Education: Selected Writings.* Edited by Reginald D. Archambault. Chicago and London: The University of Chicago Press, Phoenix Books, 1974.

————. *My Pedagogic Creed;* and Small, Prof. Albion W. *The Demands of Sociology Upon Pedagogy.* Chicago: A. Flanagan Company, 1897.

————, and McLellan, James A. *The Psychology of Number, and Its Applications to Methods of Teaching Arithmetic.* International Education Series. New York: D. Appleton and Company, 1896.

————. *The School and Society.* Revised edition. Chicago: The University of Chicago Press, 1926.

————, and Dewey, Evelyn. *Schools of Tomorrow.* New York: E.P. Dutton and Company, 1915.

Dropkin, Ruth, and Tabier, Arthur, editors. *Roots of Open Education in America.* New York: The City College Workshop for Open Education, December 1976.

DuBois, W. E. B. *Crisis* 40 (1925).

First Century of National Existence: The United States as They Were and Are. Selected subjects and authors. Hartford, Connecticut: L. Stebbins, 1872.

Franklin, Benjamin. *Proposals Relating to the Education of Youth in Pennsylvania.* Published in Philadelphia, 1749.

Goodman, Paul. *Compulsory Mis-Education and the Community of Scholars.* New York: Vintage Books, 1966.

Gross, (to come). *The Lifelong Learner.*

Hall, G. Stanley. *Aspects of Child Life and Education.* Edited by Theodate L. Smith. Boston: Ginn and Company, 1907.

————. *Educational Problems,* Volumes 1 and 2. New York: D. Appleton and Company, 1924.

Harty, Shiela. *Hucksters in the Classroom: A Review of Industry Propaganda in the Schools.* Washington, D.C.: Center for Study of Responsive Law, 1979.

Herndon, James. *In Your Native Land.* New York: Bantam Books, 1972.

————. *The Way It Spozed to Be.* New York: Bantam Books, 1969.

Holt, John. *How Children Fail.* New York: Pitman Publishing Company, 1964.

————. *How Children Learn.* New York: Pitman Publishing Company, 1967.

Hubbard, Elbert. *Little Journeys to the Homes of Great Teachers: Friedrich Froebel.* New York: The Roycrofters, 1908.

Jacks, L. P. *The Education of the Whole Man.* New York: Harper and Brothers, 1931.

Johnson, Marietta. *Thirty Years with an Idea.* University, Alabama: The University of Alabama Press, 1974.

Kozol, Jonathan. *Death at an Early Age.* New York: Bantam Books, 1968.

Lopate, Phillip. *Journal of a Living Experiment: A Documentary History of the First Ten Years of Teachers and Writers Collaborative.* New York: Teachers and Writers Collaborative, 84 Fifth Avenue, New York, New York 10011.

Mann, Mary Peabody. *Life of Horace Mann.* Washington, D.C.: National Education Association of the United States, 1937. Centennial Edition in Facsimile, reproduced from original edition published in Boston by Walker, Fuller and Company, 1865.

Marshall, Sybil. *An Experiment in Education.* Cambridge: Cambridge University Press, 1963.

McCaul, Robert L. "Dewey's Chicago." *The School Review* (Summer 1959): 258–281.

Miller, Lida Brooks. *The Kindergarten, or, Home and School Culture.* Chicago: National Publishing Company, 1891.

Monroe, Paul. *A Cyclopedia of Education,* Volumes 1–5. New York: Macmillan Company, 1911.

————, editor. *Principles of Secondary Education.* New York: Macmillan, 1914.

Monroe, Walter Scott. *An Introduction to the Theory of Educational Measurements.* Boston: Houghton Mifflin Company, 1923.

Monroe, Will S. *The Educational Labors of Henry Barnard: A Study in the History of American Pedagogy.* Syracuse, New York: C. W. Bardeen, 1893.

Mortensen, Enok. *Schools for Life.* Solvang, California: Danish-American Heritage Society, 1977.

Nearing, Scott. *The New Education: A Review of Progressive Educational Movements of the Day.* Chicago and New York: Row, Peterson and Company, 1915.

Norris School Cooperative Program. *Adult Education* 10, number 4 (June 1938).

North Dakota Study Group on Evaluation. *Reading Tests: Do They Help or Hurt Your Child.* Grand Forks, North Dakota: University of North Dakota, Center for Teaching and Learning. This booklet and other valuable inexpensive material on the problems of standardized testing can be ordered from the Study Group or from Ann Cook and Deborah Meier, 670 West End Avenue, New York, NY 10025.

Parker, Francis W. *Talks on Pedagogics.* New York: Arno Press and the *New York Times,* 1969. Originally published in New York by E. L. Kellogg and Company, 1894.

Patri, Angelo. *A Schoolmaster of the Great City.* New York: Macmillan Company, 1923.

Pestalozzi, Heinrich. *The Education of Man: Aphorisms.* Introduction by William H. Kilpatrick. Translated by Heinz and Ruth Norden. New York: Philosophical Library, 1951.

———. *Leonard and Gertrude.* Translated and abridged by Eva Channing. Boston: D.C. Heath, 1895.

Pinloche, A. *Pestalozzi and the Foundation of the Modern Elementary School.* The Great Educators series. New York: Charles Scribner's Sons, 1912.

Pintner, Rudolf. *Intelligence Testing: Methods and Results.* New York: Henry Holt and Company, 1924.

Pressey, Sidney L., and Pressey, Luella Cole. *Introduction to the Use of Standard Tests: A Brief Manual in the Use of Tests of Both Ability and Achievement in the School Subjects.* New York: World Book Company, 1922.

Proceedings of the N.E.A. meeting in Oakland, California, 1923.

Proctor, William Martin. *The Use of Psychological Tests in the Educational and Vocational Guidance of High School Pupils. Journal of Educational Research Monographs,* number 1. Bloomington, Illinois: Public School Publishing Company, 1921.

Propaganda Analysis 4, number 4 (February 25, 1941).

Rice, Joseph Mayer. *The Public School System of the United States.* New York, 1893.

Rousseau, Jean Jacques. *Emile.* Translated by Barbara Foxley. London: J. M. Dent and Sons, 1955. First published in 1911.

Rugg, Harold. *America's March Toward Democracy, History of American Life: Political and Social.* Boston: Ginn and Company, 1937.

———, and others. *The Foundations of Curriculum-Making.* New York: Arno Press and the *New York Times,* 1969. Originally published in Bloomington, Illinois, by the Public School Publishing Company, 1926.

————, and Krueger, Louise. *Communities of Men*. New York: Ginn and Company, 1936.

————, and Shumaker, Ann. *The Child-Centered School*. New York: Arno Press and the *New York Times*, 1969. American Education Series. Originally published in New York by World Book Company, 1928.

————, and others. *Curriculum-Making, Past and Present*. New York: Arno Press and the *New York Times*, 1969. American Education Series. Originally published in Bloomington, Illinois, by the Public School Publishing Company, 1926.

Scott, C. Winfield, Clyde M. Hill, and Hobert W. Burns, eds. *The Great Debate*. Englewood, New Jersey: Prentice Hall, 1959.

Shragg, Peter, and Divoki, Diane. *The Myth of the Hyperactive Child*. New York: Dell, 1976.

Smith, William Hawley. *All of the Children of All of the People*. New York: Macmillan Company, 1912.

Stonorov, Oscar, and Kahn, Louis. *You and Your Community: A Primer*. Published as a public service by Revere Copper and Brass, Inc., 1944.

Stowe, Calvin. *The Report on Elementary Public Instruction in Europe*. Columbus, Ohio: The Ohio State Legislature, 1837.

Synnott, Marcia G. "The Admission and Arsenal of Minority Students at Harvard, Yale and Princeton 1900–1950." *Journal of the History of Education* 19, number 3 (Fall 1979).

Terman, Lewis M. *The Intelligence of School Children, How Children Differ in Ability, The Use of Mental Tests in School Grading, and the Proper Education of Exceptional Children*. Boston: Houghton Mifflin Company, 1919.

————, and others. *Intelligence Tests and School Reorganization*. New York: World Book Company, 1922.

————. *The Measurement of Intelligence, An Explanation of and a Complete Guide for the Use of the Stanford Revision and Extension of the Binet-Simon Intelligence Scale*. Boston: Houghton Mifflin Company, 1916.

Thorndike, Edward L. *Handwriting*. New York: Teachers College, Columbia University, 1917.

————. *The Principles of Teaching, Based on Psychology*. New York: A. G. Seiler, 1906.

Von Marenholz-Bulow, Baroness B. *Reminiscences of Friedrich Froebel*. Translated by Mrs. Horace Mann. Boston: Lee and Shepard, 1877.

Wallace, F. C. *Rockdale*. New York: Knopf, 1978.

Wesker, Arnold. *Words as Definitions of Experience*. London: Writers and Readers Publishing Company, 1976.

Woodham-Smith, P., and others. *Friedrich Froebel and English Education*. Edited by Evelyn Lawrence. London: University of London Press, 1961. First published 1952.

Woodhull, John F. "The Aims and Methods of Science Teaching." *General Science Quarterly* 2 (November 1917): 249.